Papers presented at the
Seventh Conference on the Believers' Church
Anderson School of Theology
Anderson, Indiana, June 5-8, 1984

Baptism & Church

A BELIEVERS' CHURCH VISION

Edited by
MERLE D. STREGE
With an Introduction by John Howard Yoder

SAGAMORE BOOKS

Baptism and Church: A Believers' Church Vision
Copyright © 1986 by Sagamore Books
P. O. Box 195, Grand Rapids, Michigan 49588

Library of Congress Cataloging in Publication Data

Conference on the Concept of the Believers' Church
    (7th : 1984 : Anderson School of Theology)
    Baptism and church.

    Includes bibliographical references.
    1. Baptism and church member ship--Congresses.
2. Baptism and Christian union--Congresses.
3. Free churches--Congresses. 4. Baptism, Eucharist
and ministry--Congresses. 5. Sacraments and Christian
union--Congresses. 6. Baptism--Congresses. 7. Lord's
Supper--Congresses. 8. Clergy--Office--Congresses.
I. Strege, Merle D. II. Title.
BV820.C57 1984   234'.161   85-43567
ISBN 0-937021-00-8

Printed in the United States of America.

86 87 88 89 90 / 9 8 7 6 5 4 3 2 1

INTRODUCTION

The "Conferences on the Concept of the Believers' Church" are the product of the vision of Professor Johannes A. Oosterbaan, who had been called to represent the *Doopsgezinde* of the Netherlands in meetings of the World Council of Churches. His experiences at the New Delhi Assembly (1961) had shown him that, whereas the churches of the major magisterial traditions have solid bases (both documents and institutions) from which to enter the ecumenical arena, the churches of the Radical Reformation traditions have neither a single language nor a concerted strategy. In fact, the heirs of the various "free" renewal movements hardly even know one another.

The "concept" of which the conference series speaks is more than a single-issue dissent from mainline Protestantism, with regard to the canonical technicalities of sacramental praxis (how old the baptisand must be, how much water there must be, how baptism relates to membership, and so on), which could be measured from the baseline of said main line and in its terms. The concept is a distinctive view of what the main line of the Christian tradition is, how it is discerned, and how it takes social form. It was thus fitting that the efforts of scholars and ministers to articulate it anew should have taken a "free church" form, with no central administration, no defined captive constituency, and no regular calendar.

After attending the Faith and Order Assembly at Montreal (1963) Professor Oosterbaan began gathering support in North America for his vision. He was able to win for it the backing of the Southern Baptist Seminary which, after extensive deliberation and consultation, convened the first and largest "Conference on the Concept of the Believers'

Church" in July, 1967.[1] There the choice was made (a) to prolong the conversations and (b) to do so in the informal "free church" way which led to the 1985 seventh conference in Anderson. Each conference session had its own volunteer sponsorship, which determined program content, scope, and format, in consultation with a very loosely structured "committee on continuing conversations." It was a privilege to serve with Dr. John W. V. Smith on this committee, ever since the last planning session before the Louisville conference. It is most fitting that the seventh conference in the series should have been his own, his last major project.

It was fitting that the study of the "concept of the believers' church" should have been initiated by historians, who in recent generations have moved beyond narrative detail and apologetics to the theological task of typological analysis.[2] The historian who discerns as "concept" a set of characteristics of the way God works in renewing His people is not bringing to the facts an arbitrary grid; he is discerning the tracks of the renewing Spirit in the recurrens patternedness of restoration events ever since the first Pentecost. The nuclear agenda of the series has thus been historical, and the leading planners have been historians, like John Smith.

Yet the historians have not been uncommitted archaeologists, skeptics, and archivists. They have regularly been at the same time churchmen (and a few—too few—churchwomen) integrating their technical expertise into their ministries as pastor, teacher, and missionary—driven not by idle curiosity nor by value-free data-crunching, but by zeal for the house of the Lord. The vision they track through the renewal events of the past serves as a flexible but ever-pertinent paradigm for the present ministries to which they give themselves.

The *label* "believers' church" is only one of several. Coined by the outgroup interpreter Max Weber, its meaning is functional, not invidious. It does not suggest that other kinds of Christians are not believers, any more than the labels "reformed," "orthodox," or "catholic" should be pressed for their maximal negative implications. The more historically oriented designation "radical reformation," given currency by George H. Williams, has the shortcoming of being a context-dependent term; only where there is a "non-radical" reformation (which Williams dubbed "magisterial") does the "believers' church" concern demand "radicalization". Some "radicals" (the so-called "spiritualizers") have not wanted to form churches. Other "radicals" have mitigated the clarity of their appeal to faith by not renouncing the appeal to governmental or antigovernmental coercion. Likewise the more broadly used term "free church"[3] is context-dependent: it may designate voluntary membership, freedom from state control, or the rejection of prescribed forms of worship or belief. It negates a negation or a constraint, without naming what it affirms. "Restoration" churches or "restitution" churches, the favored designations of the Churches of God and the Churches of Christ, makes sense when describing the intention operative at the inception of a movement; but it does not describe its normative content nor the meanings of its continuity.

Increasing acquaintance with sister communions not only corrects the narrowness of our preoccupation with schismatic origins as we perceive and practice an alternative mode of Christian unity[4]; it guides us to a renewed understanding of the regular, continuing life and mission of the church. That makes this conference's attention to concrete pastoral praxis, needing to answer questions the restoration founders did not resolve, quite fitting.

The genius of the series of "Conferences on the Concept . . ." has been to avoid getting stuck with definitional agenda. Without needing to know which of the above alter-

native *labels* was most exactly adequate, there has been
sufficient common conviction about the main lines of common conviction[5] to permit the "continuing conversations"
to stride on into matters of mission and ministry ("Is there a
believers' church style of life?"—1970) as well as of doctrine
("Is there a believers' church christology?"—1980). The series thereby accepted the challenge to demonstrate that "the
believers' church" represents a global alternative orienta-
tion, around which the entire scope of theology can be
realigned.

It was thus a normal maturation of the series' mission,
once the identity statement had been clarified, that the conversation should move on to matters not traditionally perceived as denominationally "distinctive." There has in fact
been some hesitancy about attending to some of the subjective and experiential dimensions (regeneration, sanctification, discipline) which some would consider the most distinctive. This broadening into other agenda began already
with the christology conference; it began in earnest with the
Anderson event, where for the first time dialogue was formally engaged with the majority Christian traditions at the
point of our initial controversy, namely the continuing
challenge to pedobaptism.

Long a participant in interfaith meetings under the
aegis of the National and World Councils of Churches, John
Smith saw the pertinence of the new Faith and Order draft
on "Baptism, Eucharist, and Ministry" as an instrument for
serious encounter, made to order to engage some of the
points of classical free church witness. The free churches had
long claimed a special ecumenical agenda. Especially the
"restoration" movements of the nineteenth century had
bypassed the old questions of polity to resolve just that kind
of question.[6] Is there some other approach to the truth question, different both from coercive uniformity after the mag-

isterial models, and from pluralisitc inclusivism? The free church makes that claim; there are ways to disavow coercion without giving up on the truth; namely, through binding dialogue under the rule of Scripture.

The Faith and Order pilgrimage of the majority non-Roman traditions[7], as its first two generations' achievements have come to be distilled in the consensus document "Baptism, Eucharist, and Ministry," has been led—to say this is no reproach—by an ethos of compromise. There is much that can be achieved in this way. There are many ancient polarizations that can in fact be surmounted by more critical semantics. There are times and places where apparently contradictory theses are in fact complementary. Yet the ethos of synthesis cannot be imposed where a classical structural disjunction is built into the meaning of the gospel. It was thus a risky, accountable, though unpopular against-the-stream act of ecumenical responsibility when the Anderson conference began to articulate the inadequacies of the B.E.M. compromise on baptism. For that too we thank John Smith.

John Howard Yoder
University of Notre Dame

John W. V. Smith, 1914–1984
Professor Emeritus of Church History
Anderson School of Theology
Member, Conference on the Concept of Believers' Church
Member, Commission on Faith and Order
National Council of the Churches of Christ, U.S.A.

PREFACE

A few words are in order about the organization and occasion of this volume. The essays collected here were read to the Seventh Conference of the Believers' Church, which was convened June 5–8, 1984 in Anderson, Indiana. The purpose of that conference was the discussion of the Baptism section of "Baptism, Eucharist, and Ministry" (Faith and Order Paper Number III), published by the World Council of Churches. The result of the discussions of those three days was a "reception response statement," published as the third section of this book.

The chapters of this volume appear in the same sequence in which they were read as papers to the conferees. The conference designers sought a particular line of development in the conference and I have thought it important to duplicate that line in written form. In at least one respect readers of this volume will experience the same shifts and progression of ideas as those women and men who participated in the conference. Section one is thus a collection of papers examining the particular approaches to the questions of baptism and church membership of several constituencies within the believers' churches. After these appear five broader essays, commenting on the practice of pedobaptism and explaining the development of the B.E.M. reception process. Finally, in response to the Baptism section, appears the Conference statement as it was transmitted to the Faith and Order Commission Office in Geneva.

John W. V. Smith was working on the publication of these papers when he suffered a fatal heart attack in November, 1984. The completion of this, his final project, was made possible in part through the assistance of a number of his friends and colleagues in Anderson. Their names are listed elsewhere in this volume, however special acknowledgment and thanks must be expressed to the Faith and Order Commission of the National Council of Churches of Christ and its Director, Brother Jeffrey Gros, F.S.C., without whose assistance this collection would not have been published. The contributions of all testify to our love for John and the honoring of his memory by many more than those whose names appear here.

Because this volume is dedicated to John, I have been tempted to include in it some material from his own work, both published and unpublished. In the end the decision was not to include it. The project originally was John's and he certainly would not have seized such an opportunity to see his own work in print. He fervently believed that the unity of Christians is accomplished when they join in the presence of the Spirit and he worked tirelessly for many years at helping us come together. The Anderson meeting of the believers' churches was the final expression of John's beliefs about Christian unity. As they are published here, the papers of that conference testify again to those beliefs and complete his assignment as John himself would have finished it.

John Smith was teacher and colleague. His primary academic interest was the history of the Church of God (Anderson, Indiana). Out of that interest grew his collegial churchmanship. He traced the history of one communion's approach to the question of Christian unity. He practiced it in his thoroughgoing ecumenical spirit. The result was a genuine praxis of the oneness of the people of God in the life of a man many of us were privileged to name as friend and brother. In his memory this book is published.

Merle D. Strege
Anderson School of Theology

CONTENTS

SECTION I:
Baptism and Membership
In the Believers' Churches

The Mennonites

MARLIN E. MILLER

President
Goshen Biblical Seminary

The conference planners have asked me to summarize the Mennonite understanding and practice of baptism, both in their historical development and in their contemporary realities. Given the diversity of groups as well as the chronological and geographic spread of Mennonites, the scope of this presentation will need to be drastically limited. Rather than attempting a balanced survey of the entire history, I shall concentrate on the Anabaptist-Mennonite origins in sixteenth-century Europe. And rather than tracing the understandings and practices represented by all Mennonite groups, I shall focus on the strands claimed by two Mennonite groups in twentieth-century North America. These two groups, the Mennonite Church and the General Conference Mennonite Church, are numerically the two largest Mennonite bodies in the United States and Canada; they are also the two groups being represented in this conference by the Associated Mennonite Biblical Seminaries.

My remarks will consequently be divided into two major sections. The first part of this presentation will review understandings and practice during the beginnings of the Anabaptist-Mennonite groups during the early and mid-sixteenth century. The second part will report on the results of an impressionistic survey on contemporary understandings and practices among Mennonites in the mid-western United States and Ontario.[1]

I.

The formative significance of the 1527 Schleitheim Articles for the consolidation of the early Swiss and South German streams of the Anabaptist movement has been rediscovered in contemporary historical scholarship. Moreover, the Schleitheim Articles have found their way into recent North American Mennonite catechetical materials. At least one major Mennonite group, The Mennonite Church in North America, has included it in the denominational constitution as one of the confessional statements which provide a standard for membership. We may therefore appropriately begin with the Schleitheim Articles as a benchmark in an Anabaptist-Mennonite understanding of baptism and church membership. By comparison and contrast we will also be able to note some similarities and differences between sixteenth-century understandings and current North American Mennonite tendencies.

The Schleitheim Articles begin with the baptism theme. Article One reads as follows:

> Baptism shall be given to all those who have been taught repentance and the amendment of life and who truly believe that their sins are taken away through Christ, and to all those who desire to walk in the resurrection of Jesus Christ and be buried with him in death, so that they might rise with Him; to all those who with such an understanding themselves desire and request it from us; hereby is excluded all infant baptism, the greatest and first abomination of the Pope. For this you have the reasons and the testimony of the writings and the practice of the apostles.[2]

This article offers in rather concentrated form an order for understanding the baptism which characterizes a formative stream of Anabaptist life and thought. Note particularly that baptism shall be given to those:

1. who have been taught repentance and the amendment of life;
2. who believe that their sins have been removed through Jesus Christ;
3. who express their desire to walk in newness of life, namely to take up what came to be called discipleship or following Christ in life;
4. who so understand baptism, desire it, and ask for it.

This pattern repeats itself in the writings of major sixteenth-century Anabaptists such as Balthasar Hubmaier, Menno Simons, and Pilgram Marpeck. Focusing particularly on the Great Commission in both its Matthean and Markan forms they reiterate the priority of preaching/teaching, followed by a response of faith, inner regeneration, a commitment to discipleship, and baptism and a public confession of faith, or as Menno puts it, as a sign of obedience to the command of Christ. This sequence necessarily excludes the baptism of infants, who can neither respond to God's Word in faith, nor commit themselves to a life of discipleship, nor request baptism.

Article Two of Schleitheim deals with the "ban," that is the exercise of congregational admonition and discipline according to Matthew 18. The ban is to be employed "with those who have been baptized into the one body of Christ . . . and still somehow slip and fall into error and sin . . . ."[3] The next article concerns "the breaking of bread," and stipulates that those who desire to participate "must beforehand be united in the one body of Christ, that is the congregation of God. . . . and that by baptism."[4] Baptism as understood in Article One is thus directly linked to entry into the Christian church. Membership in the church is furthermore indissolubly tied to the exercise of church discipline and sharing in the Lord's Supper. Baptism on confession of faith and with the commitment to discipleship thus includes becoming a member in the church and beginning to participate in its discipline as well as to partake in communion. Baptism as a public confession of faith and a sign of obedience to Christ simultaneously means entry into a congregation of believers characterized by separateness from the evil and wickedness in the world, by sharing in a unity of spirit and love maintained by a common discipline and by a common remembrance of Christ's broken body and shed blood.

Hubmaier tied the authority to bind and loose to the baptismal pledge perhaps more explicitly and systematically than Menno, Marpeck, or other sixteenth-century Anabaptist writers or church leaders after Schleitheim.[5] Nevertheless, the linkage of baptism with entry into church membership, mutual submission in congregational discipline, and access to communion are broadly assumed and practiced in some fashion. We shall return later to this connection between baptism and church membership, which has often undergone significant modifications and has sometimes been challenged in more recent Mennonite practice.

The Anabaptist-Mennonite emphasis on baptism as a visible testimony to faith and as a sign of obedience implies a departure from sacramental views of baptism which consider it a means of grace. Mennonites often refer to baptism as a symbol to distinguish their view from sacramental views. If sacramentalist views unduly emphasize baptism as God's action and gift at the expense of prior faith and commitment, Mennonite views may frequently tend toward a "moderate spiritualism" or excessive "subjectivism." Both these tendencies and attempts to correct them in ways consistent with believers' baptism accompany both the historical and the contemporary discussion and practice among Mennonites.

In his study on *Anabaptist Baptism*, Rollin Armour has described the varying emphases among several sixteenth-century Anabaptists, ranging from the moderate spiritualism of a Hubmaier to the later, more "objective" view of Marpeck. In addition to focusing on the sequence of teaching, faith response, and baptism, Hubmaier as many others then and now, emphasized that baptism represents the pledge of a good conscience before God citing 1 Peter 3:20ff. in this regard. Marpeck however moved beyond grounding baptism only in the dominical command or describing it simply as the sign of a good conscience before God in his search to avoid both the spiritualist and the sacramental pitfalls. Marpeck shared with other Anabaptists the view that regeneration began prior to baptism and that baptism was an outer sign of the new birth. However, Marpeck went on to contend that the sign participated in the reality of regeneration.[6]

> As in all other matters, the reality must precede its own witness, so that the sign can be rightly taken or given. When otherwise, the sign is false and a vain mockery. If the reality is there and is known, then the sign is truly and wholly useful, and everything signified by the sign is [then] to be given to the sign, for it is no more a sign, but a reality.

This means that even though forgiveness of sin precedes baptism in that the Holy Spirit was already at work creating a good conscience, forgiveness is also given "in" baptism. Conceptually, Marpeck elaborated the concept of a "co-witness" in which the inner witness of the Holy Spirit is matched by an outer witness which complements it. The co-witness is by implication as valid as the inner action itself, even though it corresponds to it rather than mediating it. In addition to the notion of a co-witness, Marpeck also described the unity of baptism in terms of the action of the Trinity. According to this view, the unity of inner and outer baptism is founded in the nature of God whose inner spiritual actions in human beings are always complemented by the outward actions of Christ, or the Christian church as His successor. And finally, he offered an anthropological rationale, interpreting baptism as including both the inner and the outer aspects of the human individual.

Armour concludes that Marpeck thus understood baptism to transmit God's grace to the baptizand in a limited sense, namely as a divine word assuring the one being baptized of forgiveness and regeneration through faith. The "objective" character of the baptismal action thus means that the baptizand receives the testimony from the baptizing church that they have recognized in him or her the inner gift of the Spirit, of forgiveness, and regeneration. Because this external co-witness of the church follows and completes the inner witness of the Spirit, infant baptism is by definition excluded, as well as exegetically unfounded.

Although Marpeck sought to articulate a theology of baptism which integrated both "subjective" and "objective" dimensions, another strand has, on the whole, more broadly influenced Mennonite thought and practice over the centuries. Menno Simons may be taken as the representative voice for a more "subjective" tendency, formulated in large measure as a corrective to pedobaptist and sacramentalist views. In his *Foundation of Christian Doctrine* (1539), Menno emphasizes baptism as a "covenant of a good conscience with God."[7] In his essay on "Christian Baptism" (1539), he describes baptism as a sign of obedience which proceeds from faith, emphasizes that regeneration comes by faith in God's Word rather than by receiving the sacrament, and reiterates that baptism follows regeneration rather than effecting it.[8] Those so baptized become members of the Christian church understood as the "communion of the saints," in which a disciplined life of faith, worship, and Christian obedience—as well as suffering—are the hallmarks. In comparison to Schleitheim or Marpeck, Menno's view focuses more on the individual believer than on the corporate reality of the believing community. In his emphasis on baptism as a symbol of obedience to Christ's command, Menno gives very little attention to the "objective" side of baptism, which Marpeck also articulated in his debate with spiritualistic tendencies.

This strand took confessional shape in the Dordrecht articles of 1632.[9] It has significantly informed North American Mennonite confessional and catechetical statements, at least until recent decades. The renaissance in Anabaptist studies and the more recent use of "believers' church" typology have documented the range of views among early Anabaptists, and have sought to rehabilitate the ecclesiological, hence the corporate dimensions of baptism. The same tendencies are seeking to recapture something of the social-ethical context of Christian baptism and its "objective" as well as "subjective" aspects.

In both strands of baptismal theology, Mennonites have emphasized the corollary doctrines of "free will" and "discipleship." Sinful human beings have sufficient free will to respond to the Gospel—or to reject it. And those who confess Jesus as Lord and declare their intention to follow him in life are enabled by the Holy Spirit to live as disciples. This ethical capacity enabled by the Spirit has not been perceived as a capacity for leading a sinless life. Practically speaking, the strong emphasis on "fraternal admonition" and church discipline presupposes the continuing lack of perfection in the sense of sinlessness. Theologically, the dialectic between discipleship and the disciples' shortcomings has been articulated in several ways. Already Menno Simons phrased this tension in a manner which reflected both a certain confidence about the reality of regeneration and a measured sobriety about baptized believers: we are "not cleansed. . . of our inherited sinful nature . . . so that it is entirely destroyed, but in baptism we declare that we desire to die to it and to destroy it, so that it will no longer be master" (Romans 6:12).[10]

These understandings of baptism excluded infant baptism and implied baptizing those who have reached an age of moral awareness, who ask for baptism out of their response to Jesus Christ in faith, who commit themselves to follow Christ in faith, who commit themselves to follow Christ in life, and so become members of the Christian church. Among the Anabaptists and Mennonites in the sixteenth century, proposals on an appropriate age for baptism, assuming the faith-response and the commitment to discipleship, ranged from 7 to 30 years.[11] In the historical context of European Christendom where all had been baptized as infants, the question of age was not phrased primarily in terms of integrating a younger generation into the faith community. The experiential frame of reference was shaped by a missionary and persecuted minority which had challenged a major supporting axiom of the *Volkskirche.*

As to the mode of baptism, pouring water on the head most likely has been most broadly used, both in the early years and at the present time. However some early Anabaptist and Mennonite leaders apparently practiced baptism both by pouring and by immersion. One major Mennonite group, the Mennonite Brethren Church, practices baptism by immersion. Others either prefer and practice baptism by pouring or accept both forms, particularly in recent decades.

II.

Within the constraints of this presentation, I cannot trace the historical developments of baptism among Mennonites between the sixteenth and twentieth centuries. Painting with very broad strokes, one can perceive both similarities and changes. Generally speaking, Mennonites have sought to maintain "believers' baptism" in thought and practice. Numerous influences and challenges have however inflected both the significance and the exercise of baptism among Mennonites in North America since their coming to this continent in 1683.

One set of changes may be characterized as the routinization of baptism in the preservation of a predominantly ethnic religious community. Through a variety of expectations and practices, there was a movement toward considering the years from 15-18 as appropriate for baptism. Baptism became one among several landmarks on the way from adolescence to adulthood and marriage as well as church membership.

In more recent history, American revivalism has in part reinforced the emphasis upon believers' baptism and in part introduced new emphases into Mennonite understandings and practice. Revivalism's emphasis on conversion and a voluntary response to the Gospel renewed the view that baptism as a public sign should be preceded by a voluntary and personal faith. Revivalism's preoccupation with an individual's crisis conversion has however diminished both the direct relation between baptism and church membership and the understanding of faith as a commitment to Christian discipleship in all areas of life, both personal and social.

Together with the broader stream of revivalism, child evangelism has made some inroads into Mennonite groups in the mid-twentieth century. These influences have been most perceptible in the Mennonite Church, where young children of 4 or 5 years have been baptized. The neo-Anabaptist renaissance beginning in the late 1920s and more careful attention to children's development and nurture, particularly since the 1950s, have gradually raised the average baptismal age somewhat.[12] A survey taken during the 1970s pegged the average age for baptism in the Mennonite Church at 14; and in the General Conference Mennonite and Mennonite Brethren churches at 16 years of age.[13] Mennonites have most likely done rather well in maintaining a form of believers'—or at least youth—rather than infant baptism. Voluntary response, the obedience of faith, and "joining the church" are somehow related to the "symbol" of baptism. However Mennonites also lack a comprehensive reformulation of baptismal theology and practice in view of several historical tendencies and contemporary challenges. And the linkage between baptism and church membership may have eroded in some instances.

These tentative impressions are partly informed by a recent non-scientific survey of several Mennonite conference, congregational, and educational leaders.[14] These tentative impressions may be summarized in six major points.

First, fourteen of twenty-two respondents to the questionnaire understood baptism primarily as a symbol of conversion, pardoning and cleansing. Only one-third see baptism primarily in terms of a public commitment to Christian discipleship. The relative weight of these responses may reflect the revivalist emphasis on personal conversion with less attention to Anabaptist concerns about a commitment to walk in newness of life. Half of the respondents linked baptism to entry into the church.

Secondly, the relation between water baptism and the gift of the Holy Spirit apparently constitutes a major problem area in present understanding and practice. Only two of the twenty-two persons explicitly view baptism as a symbol for the gift of the Holy Spirit. Sixteen of the twenty-two, or over two-thirds of the respondents, favored or practiced and taught baptism by pouring, the mode which in traditional Mennonite doctrine symbolized the gift of the Spirit; only one explicitly expressed this relation. A separate question on water baptism as related to the anointing by the Holy Spirit was understood and answered primarily in reference to neo-pentecostal and charismatic currents among Mennonites. Approximately one-third (8) thought that the relation is a very close one, but an equal number considered the question a non-issue. Four persons answered that the Holy Spirit is given with conversion and three that the gift of the Spirit and water baptism are completely separate.

Thirdly, the majority (16) of the respondents continue to connect baptism directly with the beginning of church membership. That is hardly surprising; more significant may be the finding that the remaining seven did not postulate a direct link. The reasons for loosening this connection vary and are not always clear. In some cases, where baptism has been understood as a public confession of faith, the need for baptism after a public confession during revival meetings has seemed less pressing. On the other hand, baptism may be understood as related to the universal body of Christ without direct relationship to membership in the local congregation. Or in still other instances, baptism may be practiced in other than congregational settings, thus effectively diminishing the visible connection between membership in a gathered congregation and baptism. In one instance, young people see little need for becoming church members and hence for requesting baptism, because it appears to make little practical difference. They perceive church membership to differ from regular participation in Sunday services and other church activities only in two ways, namely voting at church business meetings and tithing—neither of which exercise great attraction as reasons for requesting baptism! Finally, in some congregations, baptism as the prerequisite to participation in the Lord's Supper is also being questioned. This may also effectively make baptism itself less meaningful as incorporation into the Christian church.

Fourthly, the average age for baptizing young people who have grown up as children of Christian parents in the church seems to be rising somewhat. Some reasons for this trend are most likely indebted to a renewal of Anabaptist perspectives on a voluntary faith response, commitment to discipleship, and mutual accountability in congregational life. Many ministers are encouraging this direction. Some reasons for this trend are more problematic. Postponing baptism because church membership seems less than meaningful may demonstrate a measure of integrity, but also points to serious problems in the nature of church life. The increased mobility of youth and young adults is also a factor in postponing baptism for extended periods of time after coming to faith. If baptism signifies entry into the church, some new believers hesitate to identify with a local congregation and hence to request baptism while they are pursuing their education, accepting service assignments, or beginning careers in settings other than the congregations of their parents.

Fifthly, current practices vary with respect to nurture and baptism. In some congregations, pastors schedule instructional classes for specific age groups, usually during the early teen years, as a routine teaching instrument. Those completing the period of instruction may choose whether or not to request baptism, although peer and familial pressures favor baptism as the normal outcome. In the last two or three decades however, a majority of ministers have begun to schedule the instructional classes when specific individuals request them and express interest in considering or readiness for baptism. A comprehensive reflection on and approach to nurture in the church, consistent with believers' church perspective, continues as a matter of discussion and debate rather than as a clear consensus.

Sixthly, and finally, "re-baptism" is being understood somewhat less consistently and practiced somewhat less rigorously among contemporary Mennonites than four centuries ago. In the sixteenth century, Anabaptists and Mennonites rejected the charge of rebaptism, because they considered infant baptism to be in fact no baptism. Most Mennonite groups have continued this view through the centuries. Some extended the criteria of valid baptism to include the mode as well as the faith-response of the believer. Most recently however, and as reflected in our impressionistic survey, some are more reluctant to insist that those baptized as infants need to be (re-)baptized upon confession of faith.

Five of the twenty-two respondents require baptism on confession of faith, and between nine and twelve strongly prefer it with very rare exceptions. The remainder however would give significant weight in the candidates' preference, particularly if they "resist rebaptism." In such cases there would be greater openness to ask what confirmation or baptism as an infant "means" to the candidate. Or there would be greater openness to receiving such persons into church membership if they have been living as Christians and participating actively in another congregation for some time. In situations where these persons have been received without "re-baptism," other congregational members may or may not be of a common mind on the matter.

I shall attempt no clear conclusions—particularly the impressionistic and non-scientific character of our survey would caution against conclusive statements on current Mennonite understandings and practices of baptism. Nonetheless, my impression remains that Mennonites would do well to seriously address, in a renewed and serious fashion, the whole issue of baptism. It may be that those things which ostensibly belong most obviously to our legacy of faith are in danger of erosion or of failing in part to meet present-day challenges. My hope would be that such a review and reconsideration may occur in dialogue particularly with others of the "believers' church" and with all churches who confess Jesus as Messiah, Savior, and Lord. Something like that dialogical context sparked the rediscovery of believers' baptism in sixteenth-century Europe, although "disputation" and "argument" backed by governmental authorities would be more appropriate terms than "dialogue." Something similar may contribute to parallel renewal in our time.

The Brethren

DALE W. BROWN

Professor of Christian Theology
Bethany Theological Seminary

The Brethren are cursed with and profit from the pluralism which is characteristic of American Christianity. When one paints with a broad brush a picture of where we are in our practice of something as crucial as baptism, one realizes that the strokes come out differently than if another brother or sister were painting the same landscape. With this necessary confession to historians, I proceed boldly with broad over-simplified strokes.

In an attempt to deal with both past and present in a brief space I have chosen to speak of basic shifts in the understanding of membership.

The Shift from a Counter-Culture Stance
to a More Comfortable Posture
in Relationship to the World.

No matter what the topic or text the early Brethren found their way to a discussion of baptism. We smile at this. But for them the personal decision for Christ and his body through baptism symbolized powerfully their concerns about the coercion of the state, religious freedom and the doctrine of the church as voluntary *Gemeinschaft*. In a more congenial environment, baptism gradually lost its original sociological context and became an important time of personal decision for the individual and of ingrafting of its progeny by the community of faith. Most of our present members find it difficult to empathize with those for whom baptism constituted civil disobedience. Membership in the body meant possible imprisonment, exile, and even death. This difference has led us to be much more willing to baptize our very young believers than our spiritual forefathers.

The Shift from a Discipleship to a Soteriological Focus.

Luther's debate with the Roman Catholics centered on the question, "How can I be saved?" Like the earlier Anabaptists, the Brethren seemed more preoccupied with a different question: "How can we be faithful to Jesus and his Way?" Baptism was not regarded as a guaranteed pass through the pearly gates at the time of death as much as it was personal commitment to participation in the redeeming activity of God. The Augsburg Confession accused the Anabaptists of making a human rite out of a divine sacrament. It also charged that in making faith a prerequisite for baptism, faith became a work. Therefore the Anabaptists were guilty of works righteousness. In preparing answers to these charges before a gathering of Lutheran ministers, I discovered that the first accusation could be substantiated from their perspective. The Anabaptists did not hold to a highly sacramental view of baptism. Because of this, however, the second charge was false. The early radicals claimed to be more Lutheran than Luther in maintaining that no human practices can save us, including both infant and adult baptism. They insisted that baptism did not save them for eternity. For this reason they did not worry about the eternal destination of their unbaptized children. Ultimately, it is God, not we, who seals our eternal destiny.

Out of his Pietist background, Alexander Mack was deeply concerned about questions of eternal salvation. The weight of his teachings, however, lay within the Anabaptist context. Water baptism does not save. We are saved by faith in Christ alone. But Mack hastened to add that if it be a saving faith, it will produce works of love and obedience. And to be obedient is to do what Jesus wants us to do. And that means water baptism, three times completely under.

With the influence of "methodistic" tendencies and the theology of revivalism, there early evolved a more soteriological focus in reference to baptism. Whereas it was not a concern of the early Brethren that their progeny be baptized before the early or late twenties, there came consciously and unconsciously a greater acceptance of the notion of baptismal regeneration.

In the Soviet Union orthodox priests shared with me that high communist officials would travel to remote spots where they would not be recognized to have their babies immersed three times. They still maintained they were not believers. Just in case, however, there is anything to all of this they wanted to be on the safe side. A young Brethren sister took me aside and confessed that though she was a firm believer in the Brethren way she was raised Lutheran and therefore had her baby boy christened. She added that she was not going to tell him, hoped that he would grow up and ask for believers' baptism, but just in case . . . . "Just in case," many of us have felt better about our own children being baptized at younger ages.

The Shift from Disciplined Gemeinschaft to More Inclusive Views of Membership.

We have seen that for the early Brethren baptism of someone who had been baptized as an infant constituted an act of civil disobedience. It was not long before outward signs of identity emerged such as distinctive forms of dress. For decades candidates for baptism were required to promise never to go to war. I remember my father sharing with me how he was baptized at a younger age as a result of a revival, required to wear the distinctive garb and resented being so different when enrolling in a nearby academy of the Congregational Church. With the demise of outward marks of identity and more concrete expectations of changes in life style, baptism became more of a symbol of accepting the acceptance of Christ and the community than a time of radical repentance and outward change.

Throughout all of these shifts, there have remained basic biblical themes and passages which constitute the theology of baptism among the Brethren.

First, Baptism Is Generally Associated with Conversion.

From Acts 2:38 Brethren have associated baptism with repentance and the forgiveness of sins. The early Brethren reacted to an antinomianism which they associated with Luther's emphasis on justification by faith alone. Nevertheless, the baptismal affirmations have begun with a promise to confess Jesus Christ as Lord and Savior. The candidate is baptized for the forgiveness of sins, the entire formula being, "Upon the confession of faith which you have made before God and these witnesses you are baptized for the remission of sins in the name of the Father, and of the Son, and of the Holy Spirit."

The second promise, however, moves to a call to discipleship: "Do you turn away from all sin and will you endeavor by God's grace to live according to the example and the teachings of Jesus?" It is believed that New Testament baptismal passages impart a call to discipleship. Appropriating the Pauline emphasis on dying to the old and rising to the new, we are baptized so that we might "walk in newness of life" (Rom. 6:4).

Baptism participates in both forgiving grace and enabling grace. The God who is good enough to forgive us is powerful enough to change us. Baptism signifies a conversion experience which involves both justification and regeneration. Which is emphasized more has varied according to the already alluded to historical shifts.

Second, Baptism Is a Public Covenantal Act.

For the Brethren biblical baptism is not a private decision. The covenant with God through Christ cannot be separated from the covenant with brothers and sisters. Thus the third question asked of candidates for baptism: "Will you be loyal to the church, upholding her by your prayers and your presence, your substance and your service?" The Brethren have appropriated the story in Acts 8 to suggest that baptism in the name of Jesus was not complete until Peter and John arrived from Jerusalem to lay hands on those who had received the Word of God. One does not fully receive the Holy Spirit apart from a relationship with the community of faith. The laying on of hands following baptism means that confirmation is an integral ingredient in baptism. The laying on of hands is a powerful symbol to point to the truth that the Spirit comes to us through the lives of others in the body of Christ.

Recent inquiries to our Annual conference have sought clarification as to the validity of private baptisms apart from the community of faith or the use of baptism as a symbol of purification and consecration without carrying the weight of church membership. These queries have been answered with a resounding *"no"* to any desire to separate baptism from church membership. Baptism is not complete apart from its covenantal and public character.

Third, Baptism Is Ordination to Public Ministry.

As carriers of the *"imitatio Christi"* motif, the early Brethren reflected on the meaning of baptism by looking at the example of Jesus. Alexander Mack, Jr. in his *Apology* faults the churchman for pretending that the baptism of Jesus and that of his disciples is not the same, namely, an ordination to public ministry.

> Just as the Chief High Priest pledged himself to the Father through his baptism to make the entire rebelling creation subject to Him, so all of His followers with their baptism have pledged themselves by oath to Him to assist Him in this important task. That is why Peter calls them a royal priesthood (1 Peter 2:9)[1].

Mack's biblical reference is from a passage generally considered to be a sermon preached to the newly baptized, 1 Peter 1:3 through 2:10. In a similar vein, the metaphor calling us to "put on Christ" in baptism (Gal. 3:27) suggests a stepping into ministry, comparable to the high priest's investiture with his official garb. Today, it is a New Testament scholar, Markus Barth, who has focused on this meaning. He has stressed that the baptism of Jesus constituted the beginning of his public ministry, an amazing step out of security into the midst of crowds in a conscious acceptance of entering into the ministry of the Servant.[2]

A baptismal theology of ordination may shed light on the controversy surrounding the age of baptism. The Brethren propensity to baptize adults nearer that of the age of our Lord was no doubt influenced by their conviction that the age of responsibility signaled the time to actively assume major responsibility in the community of faith. The age of baptism often coincided with the settling down in community, the arrival of the first children, the readiness to assume major economic and social responsibilities.

The movement from looking at baptism as the beginning of ordination to a time of "getting saved" can be viewed as a part of the shift from a discipleship to a soteriological paradigm. But it should be pointed out that we may need a much fuller meaning of soteriology. How would one, for example, interpret Mark 16:16, "He who believes and is baptized will be saved?" One can exegete this as being saved from hell to eternal life or again as being saved from self-centered existence to being a person for others and the kingdom coming.

It is time to look more carefully at the current debate surrounding our baptismal practices. In many places the Brethren moved to a more routine practice of membership classes for junior high age youth around which were built-in expectations that baptism and membership in the body would occur at that age. Currently, this practice is being seriously questioned in some but not in all places. In youth conferences I have had to deal with the resentment of teenagers who complain about the way they have been manipulated into baptism. In teaching Brethren beliefs at the college level, I discovered that some sixty per cent of baptized college students out of our heritage resented their baptism. It is important to remember that forty per cent did not. This is a part of a broader concern for strengthening the meaning and importance of church membership in all of our traditions. Currently the reformation mood in pedobaptist traditions is expressing itself by requiring more instruction and in many cases an older age for confirmation. In this context the Brethren are beginning to test out with one another new models for our believers' church tradition.

I have been participating in this discussion by coming as close as I ever have to imbibing insights from the current interest in developmental theories. In our tradition we appropriate the example of Jesus wherever we can. Jesus was dedicated as an infant in the temple, engaged in dialogue with the elders at the time of puberty, and was baptized in the muddy waters of Jordan to inaugurate his public ministry.

First, the time of the *birth of a new baby* in our midst is an important event in any congregation in which the church embodies community. From the beginning we have celebrated this event, if not always officially, at least unofficially as the extended family encircles the newborn at the time of the first visit to church. The Brethren more recently have adopted the practice of the presence of church parents at the time of dedication. The value of the ancient practice of godparents is recognized. For we have learned that what is often promised by the entire congregation in liturgy is not always translated into specific instances of concern which continue through the years. Some are thinking of a category such as general membership or enrollment which is inclusive of dedicated children along with others who desire to identify in some way with the congregation.

Since the *age of puberty* has been such a crucial age in the history of culture, it is reasoned that the church should not ignore it. It has been the time of *bar mitzvah*, the first communion, confirmation and baptism in religious communities. It is the time when children aspire to join the adult world, when they are anxious to do what we want them to do. For this reason it is an easy time for us to invite children to become adult members. But our most recent conference paper, adopted at Pittsburgh in 1980, made the following suggestion in response to the query about age:

> Perhaps an investigation into the recovery of the ancient practice of the catechumenate would be helpful to us. In this practice the congregation recognizes

with public ceremony those who make a decision for Christ at this age. They would be in a somewhat ambiguous position, neither outside the church nor completely within the church, but certainly within the care of the church and enjoying the benefits of its fellowship, nurture, and perhaps, the Lord's Supper. They would be entered into a program of preparation and study in anticipation of a later time of baptism.[3]

In these proposals the *rite of baptism* is not to be fixed at any particular age but would more likely correspond to what in the language of Erik Erikson would be related to working through one's identity crisis. Or it would involve the decision to turn away from a more self-centered existence and be ordained by the church for ministry and mission.

In some of the discussions there is a proposal for three stages of membership: First a general membership as in some of our church directories which list all who are related in any way to the church. Second, a membership of those who historically have been named catechumens. Hopefully, if we move this way, we will find a better word. And thirdly, an ordained membership of those who have been baptized. From this third category, the ordained baptized members, we would set aside some for special ministries in the body, namely, those who presently carry the label of "the ordained," which is another big topic for this meeting.

The Southern Baptists

TIMOTHY GEORGE

*Associate Professor of Church History
and Historical Theology
Southern Baptist Seminary*

Modern historians are agreed that the modern Baptist movement took its rise from John Smyth who, in the winter of 1609, took water from a basin and poured it over his head in the name of the Father, and the Son, and the Holy Spirit, re-baptizing himself and then his entire congregation of English Separatist refugees at Amsterdam. To his contemporaries this act of self-baptism was a shocking sacrilege which flouted even the bounds of sectarian propriety. One of his opponents said to him, "Not even the Lord Christ had done that, not even Jesus baptized himself!"[1]

In time John the Se-Baptist, as he came to be called because of his self-baptism, felt the sting of these attacks and the force of the argument that he should not have baptized himself. He then sought union with a congregation of Waterlander Mennonites in Amsterdam. The larger part of Smyth's congregation was absorbed into the Mennonite church upon his death. However, a small group led by Thomas Helwys, a layman trained in law in Lincoln's Inn, returned to London in 1612 and founded what has been rightly called the first Baptist church on English soil. And out of this small sect of English Baptists returning from Holland to England the General Baptists emerged.

By 1625 there were six General Baptist congregations scattered throughout England. They were called General Baptists because of their special emphasis on the unlimited scope of atonement. They believed that Christ had died for all and not only for the elect. And they also retained, of course, believers' baptism. It is important to say, however, that baptism was administered not by immersion but by effusion for these early General Baptists.

Another stream of English Baptists arose somewhat later and independently of these early English General Baptists. They emerged out of an independent congregation founded at London in 1616 by Henry Jacob, a radical Puritan Congregationalist. In time, this congregation also split in a number of different directions, some members questioning the validity of infant baptism, and beginning to form congregations around the principle of believers' baptism. Richard Blunt, one of the leaders of this movement, thought that baptism "ought to be by dipping the body into the water, resembling burial and rising again."[2] He was sent to the Netherlands where he observed firsthand the practice of immersion as carried out by the Anabaptist Collegiants. Upon his return to England, Blunt introduced this mode of baptism to his followers. Within a few years, immersion became the universal mode of baptism among both the General Baptists, with their Arminian theology, and the Particular Baptists, as they came to be called, because of their idea that Christ had died only for the elect.

In 1644 the Particular Baptists published the first Baptist confession of faith in England, the *London Confession,* in which the following statement on baptism is given:

> The way and manner of the dispensing of this Ordinance the Scripture holds out to be dipping or plunging the whole body under water: it being a signe, must answer the thing signified, which are these: first, the washing the whole soule in the bloud of Christ: secondly, that interest the Saints have in the death,

> buriall, and resurrection; thirdly, together with a con-
> firmation of our faith, that as certainly as the body is
> buried under water, and riseth againe, so certainly
> shall the bodies of the Saints be raised by the power of
> Christ, in the day of the resurrection, to reigne with
> Christ.[3]

This was a radical act in England in the 1640s. Thomas
Edwards, Presbyterian polemicist, was greatly shocked at
this practice of baptism by immersion. In one of his writings
he issued the following: "Whosoever re-baptized any that
had been formerly baptized should be immediately cast into
the water and drowned."[4] As a matter of fact, few if any
English Baptists were drowned in the seventeenth century,
unlike the Anabaptists on the continent in an earlier period.
However, as their meetings were illegal, many of them spent
time in prison and some died there during the years of
persecution prior to the Act of Toleration of 1689.

The Particular Baptists were Calvinist in theology.
They were generally better educated and more successful
than the General Baptists. In 1689 they published the *Second
London Confession* which was modeled on the Westminster
Confession of 1649. This became the standard confessional
document of these English Baptists.

The first Baptists in America who organized themselves
into an association, and who published a confession of faith,
emerged from the Particular Baptist movement of seven-
teenth-century England. The Philadelphia Baptist Association was organized in 1707. The Baptists flocked around
Philadelphia and Pennsylvania because it was one of the few
colonies to allow a measure of religious liberty and toleration. And in 1742 they published the *Philadelphia Confession of Faith*, the first major confession of faith of Baptists in
America. Interestingly enough, this document was printed

by Benjamin Franklin who may not have taken much time to read what he was printing on that particular occasion!

The *Philadelphia Confession* was identical with the *Second London Confession* of 1689 with the exception of two articles. One of these permitted hymn singing: hymns and spiritual songs were allowed to be sung along with the Psalms. And the second article which differed from the earlier confession required the laying on of hands for everyone who had been baptized. This was a recovery of the practice of the early church in which confirmation was originally a part of the act of baptism. Unfortunately, the practice of the laying on of hands on baptized Christians has fallen out of practice among most Baptists in America today. From Philadelphia the Calvinist Baptist tradition spread to the South, especially to Charleston. Charleston became the organizing center of the Regular (Calvinist) Baptists who would form one of the major constituencies of the original Southern Baptist Convention.

A second movement of Baptists arose indigenously in this country out of the Great Awakening, out of New England Congregationalism. The great revival preaching of George Whitefield and others had awakened many to a new found faith. In time these New Light Congregationalists, as they were called, came to accept believers' baptism along with regeneration by the Holy Spirit as necessary for membership in the church. Thus the New Light Congregationalists became the New Light Baptists. Whitefield, upon hearing of this denominational realignment, quipped that he was surprised that so many of his chicks had become ducks.

To this day, in countless little villages in Massachusetts, Vermont, and New Hampshire, one can find a white-framed Baptist church on one side of the village green and its duplicate—a Congregational church—on the other side. This reflects the schism that occurred in New England in the eighteenth century between the New Light Congregationalists and the New Light Baptists. Roland Bainton used to say that they had all begun as new lights and now have become twilights! Sadly, most of them have dwindled in number to very small congregations.

A large number of these New Light Baptists felt a call to go south to Virginia, North Carolina, and Georgia, where they planted churches and forged a new tradition. The Separate Baptist tradition began to emerge, much less influenced by confessions, much less influenced by denominational structure. To some extent, the Southern Baptist Convention is an amalgamation of these two traditions, the Charleston-Philadelphia Calvinist tradition, and what we might call the Sandy Creek tradition named after the first great center of the Separate Baptist Awakening movement in the South at Sandy Creek, North Carolina.[5]

The Southern Baptist Convention was founded in 1845. The issue of slavery was the immediate point of division between the Baptists of the North and the South. The following century was a period of denominational growth, institution building, and theological controversy. Significantly in the 1920s and 1930s, when most mainline American denominations were fractured by the fundamentalist-modernist controversy, Southern Baptists did not split. They remained together as a cohesive group, centered around the themes of missions and evangelism. However, during the last twenty years, the Southern Baptist Convention has been undergoing a terrific theological and church political controversy over many of the same issues that were prominent in the early part of our century. And I would say the greatest change in the twentieth century for Southern Baptists has been the move from a rural base in the South to a much more urban, a more pluralistic and a more secular kind of environing culture. One of the recurring debates within the Southern Baptist Convention is whether or not to change the name of the Convention. The major problem seems to be the lack of a good alternative name. The American Baptists have already captured that one. Someone has suggested Continental Baptists, others have suggested Universal Baptists. This is a constant problem because Southern Baptists have reached beyond the bounds of the region which gave them birth. This has created some particular problems with respect to baptism and church membership. I want to focus now on five pastoral problems that are especially acute for Southern Baptists and perhaps for many other Baptists as well.

(1) The first one is *the legacy of Landmarkism*. We might refer to this as Baptist successionism, the idea that there is an unbroken line of true Baptist churches extending back through the centuries to Jesus himself or, even further, to John the Baptist and the Jordan River. The immediate context of this theory was the nineteenth-century frontier where denominational rivalry was intense. All the great denominations could point to some notable founder. The Lutherans had Luther, the Presbyterians had Calvin and Knox, the Methodists had Wesley, even the Mormons had Joseph Smith. Who did the Baptists have? We didn't have anybody. Of course, the answer to that was that we had a far greater founder than any of the other denominations. We would claim Jesus himself as our founder. This was a very popular idea and it had a great deal to do with the practice of baptism.

The logic of Landmarkism went like this: The local church is the kingdom of God on earth. The only true church is a Baptist church. And therefore, only baptism duly performed in a Baptist church is true baptism. Here was not only an insistence on believers' baptism, but also an insistence on believers' baptism by Baptists. Any other baptism, even if it were by immersion, would not be acceptable. In fact, the rather opprobrious term, "alien" immersion, was coined to signify the baptism of those who had been immersed in other than Baptist traditions.

A popular expression of this ecclesiology was set forth in a novel entitled, *Theodosia Ernest*. Written in 1856 by A. C. Dayton, this book was intended to be a kind of Sunday afternoon reading on the back porch in the South.

"Mother, have I ever been baptized?" The questioner was a bright, intelligent, blue-eyed lad, some thirteen summers old. The deep seriousness of his countenance and the earnest, wistful gaze with which he looked into his mother's face showed that, for the moment at least, the question seemed very important to him. "Certainly, my son," his mother said. "Both you and your sister were baptized by the Reverend Doctor Fisher when I united with the church. Your sister remembers it well. She was six years old. You were too young to know anything about it. Your Aunt Joan says it was the most solemn ceremony she ever witnessed and such a prayer as the good old Doctor made for you I never heard before." "But Mother," rejoined the lad, "sister and I have been down to the river to see a lady baptized by the Baptist minister who came here last month and commenced preaching in the schoolhouse. They went down into the river and he plunged her under the water, quickly raised her out again, and sister says if that was baptism, then we were not baptized, because we stood on the dry floor of the church and the preacher dipped his hand into a bowl of water, sprinkled a few drops on our foreheads. She says cousin John Jones was not baptized either. For the preacher took a little pitcher of water and poured a stream on his head. Sister says she don't see how there can be three baptisms when the Scripture says one Lord, one faith, one baptism. And if there's only one, why don't they just look into the New Testament and see what it is. If the Testament says sprinkle, then it's sprinklin'; if it says pour, then it's pourin'; if it says dip, then it's dippin.' I mean to read the New Testament and see if I cannot decide which it is for myself."[6]

This is the beginning of the novel and, of course, it goes through the whole quest for true baptism which culminates in the baptism of this blue-eyed young lad of thirteen summers by the Baptist minister in the river.

Baptism was an important plank in Landmark ecclesiology. The tradition that baptism is the door to the local church has led to relative degrees of acceptance of other baptisms by Baptist churches. We can identify six major different positions which are held by different Baptist churches regarding the acceptance of baptism other than Baptist baptism.[7]

The most radical Landmark view would require rebaptism when a person moves from one local church to another. This is, after all, the logical extension of the idea that the local church is the protector and curator, in some sense, the owner, of the ordinance of baptism. Second, there are some churches that receive only persons baptized in Southern Baptist churches, a kind of denominational Lankmarkism. Third, many Southern Baptist churches receive persons baptized in other bodies that are named Baptist, although again, there would be some equivocation; some Southern Baptist churches would be reluctant, for example, to receive American Baptist baptism because of the association with the National Council of Churches. Fourth, some Baptist churches receive members who have been immersed on confession of faith in any denomination. Fifth, some Southern Baptists receive all persons baptized as believers, regardless of mode. They would insist on believers' baptism, but not necessarily on immersion. And sixth, the most radical view, open membership which would receive all persons baptized in any Christian context, including even infant baptism. There are but a few Baptist churches in the South (certainly more in the North and in England) which would hold to his practice. The issue of baptismal reception is increasingly a problem for Baptists in an ecumenical context, and sometimes even in an intra-Baptist fellowship context.

(2) The second pastoral problem I want to mention, focusing now on Southern Baptists especially, is the question of *the proper age for baptism.* Since World War II, as Southern Baptists have become more urbanized and more secularized as a denomination, the average age for baptism in Southern Baptist churches has steadily declined. It now stands at eight. Last year Southern Baptist churches baptized more than 900 children ages five and under. We might say that while we do not practice infant baptism, we have "toddler" baptism. This is a break with Baptist tradition as it has been practiced through the centuries and even with Baptist practice in Europe and England today where sixteen or eighteen is more usually the acceptable age for baptism.

The pattern of early child baptism reflects an evolution of Southern Baptists from a sectarian denomination toward what church historian E. Glenn Hinson has called a "Catholic phase of our history." We are no longer a struggling, persecuted sect. We are the majority in the fastest growing region in the United States, the sun-belt. We are one of Martin Marty's "empires of religion" in the United States. Indicative of this is the fact that the home of the President of The Southern Baptist Theological Seminary in

Louisville, a beautiful, stately mansion, was once owned by the Episcopal bishop of Kentucky! By baptizing younger and younger children who may have a love for Jesus, and may even be able to make some elementary profession of faith, are we not moving toward a position of infant baptism without confirmation?

(3) A third point has to do with *the practice of re-baptism.* Here I refer not to re-baptizing persons who come from other denominations, the Landmark question, but rather to a recent trend in Southern Baptist churches. In the process of an evangelistic service, or perhaps through introspective soul-searching, many church members come to believe that they have never had a genuine conversion experience at all. They have been baptized, perhaps been in the church for many years, perhaps have even served as deacons, Sunday School teachers, but they discover they have never really been converted. Whereupon, they make another profession of faith and are then re-baptized upon this now allegedly genuine, authentic confession and conversion. We should not disparage this practice entirely because, if we take *believers'* baptism seriously, then we must presuppose that a genuine experience of conversion and regeneration will precede baptism. However, this is a dangerous trend because it can lead very easily to an attenuation of the meaning of baptism itself. It becomes a rite of rededication rather than a rite of initiation into the Christian community. And indeed, there are a number of churches that have re-re-baptized people, again and again and again. This is a practice which undercuts our traditional and theological understanding of baptism.

(4) The fourth point concerns *the baptismal rite itself.* When we look at the early church, a document like the *Apostolic Constitutions* of Hippolytus, or Cyril of Jerusalem's *Catechetical Lectures*, we see the elaborate ceremony

and ritual that baptism involved. First of all, a period of catechism was required. Hippolytus suggested three years. Then was stipulated a serious period of preparation prior to baptism, usually during the Lenten season. The gesture of renunciation, the credo, the divestiture of clothing, the triple immersion, the laying on of hands, the oil, the celebration of the first communion—all of this was a part of a unified sacramental process in the early church. It seems that Baptists in particular have attenuated the rite of baptism. Because of our supposedly symbolic understanding of this rite, it is tempting to make it less significant and less important than it was in the early church or even in the New Testament. Let me suggest four or five ways that Baptists can overcome this liturgical loss.

First of all, emphasize the period of catechism. There needs to be an extended time of serious instruction prior to baptism, if we are to take believers' baptism seriously. And we must make baptism again the profession of faith. It is very common in many Baptist churches for an individual to come forward and be received by the pastor, and for the church to vote immediately on this person's membership. Perhaps a week or so later the person may be baptized without making any personal, audible pubic profession of faith. We need to recapture baptism as this central moment of confession. Baptism is the confession of faith, not walking the aisle or joining the church by vote, but a public profession to be done, ideally, in the baptistry itself as a part of the baptismal act.

Also emphasize the trinitarian nature of baptism. Some Baptists still practice trine immersion, as, of course, the early church did. We need not insist on this in a legalistic way, but to emphasize baptism in the name of the Father, and the Son, and the Holy Spirit is one of the things that binds Baptists and pre-church Christians with the larger Catholic and

Orthodox communities of faith. We can emphasize this in better ways than we have done.

The laying on of hands which again, as mentioned earlier, is a very important part of the early Baptist experience in America, is a kind of universal ordination. It is a liturgical enactment, if you will, of the priesthood of all believers.

Baptize out of doors, if possible. This is a New Testament practice (cf. Acts 8:26 ff.) and is recommended in the *Didache* as well. Some Baptist churches have installed a kind of baptistry that I regard as blasphemous. The candidate enters into the baptistry and sits on a reclining chair, and the minister stands behind a plastic shield, never having to enter the water. He simply reaches over and submerges the candidate in the reclining chair! It would be much better to go back to an outdoor ceremony in creeks and rivers and lakes. This would help to make baptism again a significant, liturgical event in the life of the believer.

(5) My final comment has to do with *baptismal theology*. Southern Baptists and Baptists in general have stressed the negative aspect of sacramentalism. We have stressed that baptism does not wash away sins, that it is "merely" a symbol. We have done this largely in reaction to Roman Catholic and Campbellite sacramental views. But I think we have overdone it. We need to affirm that while baptism is not a magical rite which washes away our sins, it is nonetheless a very important, sacred and serious act of incorporation into the visible community of faith. Not only are we saying something to God in baptism, but God is also saying and doing something for us in baptism. We can do this in a way respects the integrity of our own theological tradition and yet incorporates the richness of what Paul meant in the New Testament when he talked about being baptized into Christ and putting on Christ as a significant act of Christian identification.

Baptism also needs to be related more directly to the church covenant. Those who have practiced pedobaptism have had a strong communal doctrine of baptism, a strong sense of the community of faith. Those of us who practice believers' baptism have sometimes missed out on that, stressing instead the importance of individual faith and profession. But the church covenant is a focus of commitment to the community into which one enters. This is the question of baptism representing a radical lifestyle, a recovery of a much more Anabaptist view of baptism, where not only faith but repentance as well is an important dimension of baptism. We need to speak, if we are to be theologically consistent, not only of believers' baptism, but also of repenters' baptism. Only in this way can we rediscover the significance of baptism as a decisive, life-transforming transition from decay and death into the newness of life in our Lord Jesus Christ.

The Church of God (Anderson, Indiana)

A. History

MERLE D. STREGE, Th.D.

Associate Professor of Historical Theology
Anderson School of Theology

Mrs. Sarah Smith (1822–1908) was one of the early members of the Church of God Reformation Movement.[1] Along with four other persons she was enlisted as a member of Daniel S. Warner's (1842–1895) evangelistic company. The purpose of this band was the proclamation of a return to the unity and holiness of the New Testament church. In 1880 Warner had begun publishing a paper, *The Gospel Trumpet*, to spread this message. In a brief reminiscence, Mrs. Smith, whose charismatic effect on other Church of God folk is attested by her sobriquet, *"Mother in Israel,"* describes a vision of God wherein the corruption of denominational Christianity was revealed to her. In her vision she saw a large heap of rotten and moldy fruits and vegetables, the most offensive pile imaginable. But on top of the pile was a beautiful ripe pear, upon which no blemish could be seen. Thinking to save the pear, Mrs. Smith attempted to pluck it from the heap. But as she picked it up, the pear burst in her hands for it was rotten within. To Mrs. Smith the vision signified the rottenness of denominational Christianity and the especially deceptive corruption of "professed holiness people in the sects," who

had the appearance of holiness, but whose continued participation in the sin of rending the body of Christ made them
no better than the anti-holiness preachers of denominational Christianity.[2]

I.

Mother Smith's vision graphically illustrates early
Church of God thought about the nature of the church and
church membership. In the words of D. S. Warner, "The
church is 'one family in heaven and earth,' named from the
Father. Eph. 3:15. This family is 'the household of God.'
Eph. 2:19. Then it follows that only the sons of God, such as
are born of the Spirit, are in the church. And we are told that
'he that commiteth sin is of the Devil;' and 'whosoever is
born of God doth not commit sin.'. . . there are no sinners
in the church."[3] Denominational Christians and "sect-
preachers" were rotten fruit because their participation in
humanly devised denominational structures usurped God's
right to rule the church through Christ. Furthermore, they
sinned against the body of Christ by dividing it, thereby
creating a Babel of confusion.

In D. S. Warner's thought the divinely appointed means
of entering the church was, to use his term, "salvation."
Warner employed that term according to the understanding
worked out and articulated in the post-Civil War phase of
the American holiness movement. Salvation accordingly is
twofold, comprising an initial work of grace, justification,
and secondly, sanctification—". . . standing, or stablish-
ing grace; which is of perfect heart holiness." "This salvation makes us perfect."[4] For D. S. Warner it was also salvation which admitted people to the church. Since this
salvation included freedom from the sin of denominationalism, he insisted that true believers "come out" of this Baby-

lonian confusion into the Church of God Reformation Movement.

Theological works published by Church of God ministers and writers in the decades after Warner's death modified his theology of church membership. The two most important of these modifications were a shift from Warner's insistence on a *sanctified* membership to the conception of a *regenerate* membership and, secondly, the ultimate rejection of Warner's "come-outism" in favor of a conception of the local church which was controlled by ideas associated with the universal church. Come-outism no longer was regarded as necessary, since every true Christian in the world was regarded as a potential member of the local congregation.

In the first systematic theology written by a Church of God theologian, R. R. Byrum (1889–1980) describes the church, "in the broadest sense," as consisting ". . . of the aggregate of all those who have been regenerated."[5] The joining of individuals to Christ in the new birth simultaneously joins them to each other. As Byrum flatly stated the matter, "Regeneration is the method by which the Spirit of God inducts or sets members in the church."[6] In this assertion that regeneration is the door to church membership, one must recognize an important modification of D. S. Warner's original position. While Byrum may have articulated the modification with greater clarity than other Church of God theologians of his generation, he certainly was not alone in that view. H. M. Riggle (1872–1952) asserted that "the new birth is the only means of entering into the Kingdom of God (John 3:5) and the church is the visible form of Christ's kingdom here on earth."[7] F. G. Smith (1880–1947) and A. F. Gray (1886–1969) shared Riggle's conviction that the church's nature was spiritual and therefore "becoming a member in the spiritual body of Christ is necessarily a spiritual operation."[8] It is unclear whether these four individuals intentionally substituted regeneration for sanctification as the door into the church. Some of them, notably Smith, used interchangeably such terms as *conversion, regeneration,* and *salvation.*[9] It does not appear that they used the terms with Warner's precision. Whether intentional or not, the net effect of these restatements was to reinforce the idea that the Church of God is "where the Christian experience makes you a member," a slogan repeated on the letterheads of countless congregations in the United States and Canada.

The "Christian experience" of repentance and faith in Christ for the forgiveness of sin is not restricted to those who worship in Church of God congregations. More than any other figure in Church of God history, Charles E. Brown (1883–1971), fourth editor of *The Gospel Trumpet,* recognized that fact and made it an operating principle in his theology and practice of church membership. For Brown, ". . . a true christian is immediately a member of any true church which he may visit . . ."[10] Brown's vision of the local congregation as the visible expression of the church universal was shared by Earl L. Martin (1892–1961), first dean of Anderson School of Theology, whose approving quotation of the following words aptly summarizes the opinion of these later revisers of an earlier viewpoint. The church is "'the company of all those in every age who are joined to Christ in faith and love, and who labor for the ends which he seeks.'"[11]

One might summarize the history of the Church of God's doctrine of church membership as a shift from a conception of a very exclusive church and correspondingly restrictive definition of church membership to a more inclusive conception of the church and less restrictive definitions of church membership. But one should not conclude that the Church of God movement *in toto* has followed this path. Various elements in the movement have followed one or another, or some combination of individuals mentioned above, as well as others, so that *diversity* on secondary matters associated with the doctrine of church membership exists within a generally held conviction that the new birth marks the beginning of church membership. We shall now see this phenomenon of diversity within general agreement expressed in the movement's doctrine of baptism.

II.

Early in its history the Church of God movement perceived itself as a divinely initiated movement, the purpose of which was the restoration of New Testament church unity and holiness. Before D. S. Warner's death the Church of God developed a *raison d'etre* based on a church-historical exegesis of biblical apocalyptic literature. Early Church of God statements on baptism reflect the judgment that after the year A. D. 270 the church had fallen into apostasy; infant baptism was one of the marks of its fallenness.[12] Faith and repentance were regarded as the only two conditions for baptism, and since infants could not meet those criteria they were illegitimate baptismal candidates. On this point Church of God sources are in universal agreement. Another common objection to pedobaptism was born in the Church of God's legacy in American revivalism: "Those baptized in infancy too often trust in that baptism as a means of salvation and therefore fail to get awakened to the necessity of repenting sin and believing on Christ for salvation."[13]

Even a modest examination of Church of God discussions of baptism reveals that the matter of greatest concern to our tradition has been neither the importance or purpose of baptism, but rather the mode in which this rite is administered. And this heavy emphasis leads to a rather sharp and ironic contradiction. While substituting the word *ordinance*

for *sacrament,* some Church of God writers have so emphasized immersion that they seem to equate form and substance
as did some of those they criticized. H. M. Riggle expressly
argued on grammatical grounds that only immersion was
baptism; ". . . sprinkling and pouring . . . cannot be."[14]
This quasi-sacramentalism was buttressed by Riggle's position that baptism is a condition of salvation.[15] Riggle's is an
extreme position not commonly held among Church of God
ministers, therefore its presence is remarkable within a
group that has generally understood baptism as the witness
of believers. Nevertheless, the movement's high regard for
the practice of immersing believers has also sanctioned the
practice of rebaptism.[16] Clearly, Church of God writers have
attempted to authenticate a doctrine of immersion rather
than a doctrine of baptism.

Given the Church of God's long-standing commitment
to the idea of church membership through regeneration, the
idea of gaining entrance to the church through baptism has
been thoroughly and often repudiated.[17] But if baptism is for
believers only and not the doorway into the church, what are
its purpose and significance? Other than Riggle, whose
views in this area are somewhat atypical, Church of God
writers and theologians have answered such questions only
with some difficulty. They all agree that baptism is important, but the reasons for its importance vary widely and give
the reader an impression of labored reasoning.

The commonest reason given for baptism's importance
is its function as a symbolic witness of the believer's participation in the death, burial, and resurrection of Christ. The
believer witnesses to God, the church, and the world of
oneness with Christ as the Apostle Paul discusses it in
Romans 6.[18] This witness testifies to the new birth and is
especially pleasing to God as an expression of our obedience
and willingness to follow after Jesus' example.[19] Baptism,

for some, also symbolically witnesses to the washing of the soul in regeneration.[20]

Beyond the category of witness, baptism is important for some Church of God writers for its psychological effects on the individual receiving it. Baptism "reminds the believer that now he belongs to God [and] motivates [faithful discipleship] by calling attention to the follower that he is a participant in Christ's suffering, death, burial, resurrection, and new life."[21]

This brief overview might conclude by observing that despite the fact that, in the Church of God communion, baptism's importance has been stated largely in symbolic and psychological categories, some of our theologians have proceeded to discuss the criteria of a "valid" baptism. R. R. Byrum declared that baptism's ". . . essentials are: (1) that the subject by truly regenerated; (2) that he be entirely immersed in the water; (3) that he be immersed in the water in the name of the Trinity, or of Christ, and emmersed therefrom; (4) that the subject believe the administrator to be a Christian. . . . Only as baptism meets these requirements is it valid."[22] Many, I think, in the Church of God would agree with Byrum; few would pause to consider the question, "What have we *validated*?"[23]

B. Practice

WILLIAM P. SOETENGA

Pastor, The Church of God at West Anderson
Anderson, Indiana

I have intentionally chosen to deal first with the meaning of church membership. In the Church of God there exists the conviction that incorporation into the church as a member of the body of Christ takes place at the moment one confesses with the mouth and believes in the heart that God raised Jesus from the dead (Romans 10:9, 10). Membership is the consequence of spiritual experience, not an ecclesiastical decision. When one participates in the blood of Christ, receives His Spirit, and acknowledges Him as Lord, that person is a member of the church.

Our continued avoidance of formal church membership is born out of our strong conviction that the unity of the Church demands that we realize our identity with all those who are a part of the Church universal (Ephesians 23:11–22), and that the Lord adds members to His household as they are being saved from their alienation from Him and are experiencing a saving relationship with Him (Acts 2:42).

As a practitioner in the Church of God I recognize that our insistence that the meaning of church membership lies in its spiritual nature and is realized through confession and belief is not without problems. Our approach to church membership frees us from the burden of judgmentalism and makes possible a freer intercourse with the whole body of Christ. At the same time, it makes us vulnerable to an acceptance of persons without the demands of accountability.

There are congregations among us who have recognized this inherent difficulty and have moved in the direction of requesting a degree of accountability as a requirement of membership. This is particularly welcome, and any approach to church membership that does not involve accountability is a travesty. Every member has been gifted by God for the good of all and needs to be held accountable for that stewardship (1 Cor. 12:7). All members must come to grips with their need to be involved in the declaration of praise to Him who called them out of darkness into light (1 Peter 2:9). Every member needs to understand that life in Christ can only be maintained by keeping the classic disciplines of the Church (Acts 2:42). Every member needs to have a working knowledge of the faith that was delivered to the saints (Jude 3). The spiritual nature of membership will not long exist without a means of providing practical accountability for the membership of the Church.

Emphasizing the spiritual nature of membership has resulted in a problem that grows out of a sociological need persons have to feel that they belong. Our approach to Church membership has given us difficulty when it comes to practical ways of helping people to feel accepted to the local Church. We claim to reach our hands in fellowship to every blood-washed one, but have had difficulty in reaching our hand in welcome to a person in front of the worshipping church for fear that it might appear as though we were formally accepting him or her as a member. It is important that we welcome the stranger and help that stranger to feel accepted (Matthew 25:35). In some of our churches there is a growing freedom to receive church letters from other communions, and to keep those letters on file. This gives the transferring person a sense of having been accepted and received by the local church with which he or she is affiliating. Our churches are using a variety of ways to give new people a sense of belonging. Some of these include: extending the right hand of fellowship to people transferring to the local church; sharing a biographical sketch with an accompanying statement that this person or family is affiliating with the church; placing names, biographical information, and pictures on a new member bulletin board in the church narthex.

Still another weakness inherent in our position on membership may be at the point of obedience. This is a point at which membership and baptism intersect. When persons repent of sin, experience the forgiveness of God, and acknowledge Jesus as Lord, they are recognized as members of the Church of God. As a rule we do not insist that a person follow the Lord in baptism, though we strongly recommend it. Persons are neither brought into membership in the local congregation through baptism nor are they excluded from membership if they are not baptized. It is difficult to read the biblical instances of baptism without concluding that baptism was demanded of believers in apostolic times. It was not an option; baptism was a required act of obedience. It is significant to note that in most instances baptism preceded the reception of the Holy Spirit (excepting the case of Cornelius, Acts 10:48). This order of spiritual growth indicates the necessity of continual obedience. As a person received Christ and followed Him obediently in baptism, that person was opened to the experience of the deepening relationship with the Spirit of God which is the life of sanctification (Acts 2:38, 41; 8:12, 17). When we do not demand obedience as a condition of membership we are creating a fellowship that does not have fellowship with God. Generally, then, we urge the experience of baptism as a step of obedience, but we do not make it a requirement of salvation. The administration of baptism might occur at the request of someone who has recently been saved, after several conversions have occurred in a relatively short span of time, following a pastor's class experience, or at pre-determined times during the church year. When such baptismal services are planned, statements will be made from the pulpit and written as announcements in newsletters and worship folders. The message conveyed is, "You are invited to follow the Lord in baptism if you have trusted in Christ as Savior and are following Him as Lord." The stress is on "invited" and there is an absence of "required." But those of us who as practitioners have not required baptism may well be encouraging disobedience. When we do not demand obedience, even as it pertains to the baptismal confession, we may well be short-circuiting the channels through which God grants the fullness of His Spirit.

It is important to see baptism as an act of obedience and to state that there is a close relationship between obedience expressed through baptism and the experience of God's blessing and life (John 14:21). There is more involved than the presentation of a declarative, symbolic, action-word when one is baptized. The commonly held view among us is that baptism declares outwardly an inward reality. Baptism represents a sermon whose subject is God's cleansing and resurrecting power. It is a symbolic word of testimony to God's grace and a believer's incorporation into the body of Christ. Baptism, to be sure, is a declared word and a confessed testimony; but that is not all there is to the ordinance of baptism. Since baptism is an act of obedience, and because God is faithful in His response to our obedience, it also is a means of grace. All that baptism represents—fellowship in Christ's death and resurrection, cleansing from sin, reception of the Holy Spirit of God, membership in the body of Christ, renewal of the Spirit, and the promise of the Kingdom of God—is more fully realized and internalized by the one entering the waters of baptism because God is faithful in His response to obedience and faith.[1]

While emphasizing the faithfulness of God in extending His grace to the baptized believer, we do not want to lose sight of the activity of God in communicating with power the word being declared through the act of baptism. Baptism is a confession. The act of baptism expresses a person's experience of cleansing and resurrection in Jesus Christ. At this juncture in the life of the church this confession of faith is important, especially in light of the decreasing use of the altars in our churches as a place where public confession is made to newfound faith in Christ. Baptism is important to the believer as a means of expressing his or her confession. And it is important to those who witness the expression of the symbolic word-action. Surely God will not allow the word expressed through the testimony of baptism to return to Him without effect any more than He allows the word that proceeds from His mouth to return to Him empty, or the Word that was with Him at the beginning and lived in flesh among us, "full of grace and truth," to fail in achieving the purpose for which the Word was sent (Isa. 55:11; John 1:1, 14).

According to Paul in his letter to the Romans, baptism represents an identification with Christ in His death and resurrection (6:1 ff.). The death represents a dying to selfish, carnal interests and entanglements; the resurrection a vivification to a life responsive to Christ, His Spirit and purposes. In the church today, where culture, patriotism, and faith are so intermingled, one wonders whether this clear-cut death and resurrection can be precisely defined in the life of the baptized believer, and whether the representation is only symbolic. In the Church of God, where there are now more adherents outside the United States, the practice of baptism in other countries still represents a real and dramatic break with an old life apart from Christ and an initiation into the new life in Christ. In Islamic countries, according to Lester

Crose, former missionary in Lebanon and former executive secretary of the Missionary Board of the Church of God, baptism usually marks the end of a person's association with family and sometimes the end of his business interests. The sharp break with culture, occupation, and family represents a real death; the motivating factors of spirit, faith, and faith community stimulate a new existence. In a secular society like the United States, where God is either denied, ignored, or mocked, and where the values and lifestyle are anything but Christian, the word of testimony spoken through the symbolic action of baptism should be as powerful as in any non-Christian society.

Baptismal practice in Kenya suggests another way in which the Church of God has attempted to bring a correspondence between the actual experience of the adherent and the representation of repentance through baptism. A year of waiting is observed by Kenyan converts during which time they are required to prove their repentance while their spirits are being disciplined through study and worship. The result of this process is that baptizands are persons whose lives demonstrate the fruits of repentance. The unique setting of the Kenyan baptismal service also provides for a demonstration of unity through the ordinance. In a river renamed "Jordan" west of Nairobi, near Kisumu and our Kima station, there is a mass baptismal service once a year. Normally two to four hundred new believers are baptized by numerous ministers working simultaneously in the river. The unity of the Church of God in Kenya takes on new meaning in the waters of the "Jordan River." Paul's words to the Galatians come to mind: ". . . for all of you who were baptized into Christ . . . are all one in Christ Jesus," (Gal. 3:27, 28).

Further reflection on baptism as confession involves us thinking in about the context in which baptism takes place in the United States. When confession is made through baptism it is now a confession made almost exclusively to other believers. Baptism is a confession of one's break with the world and one's vivification in Christ. But this confession is appropriately made to and in the world out of which the new Christian has come. We have every reason to believe that baptism recorded in *The Acts of the Apostles* occurred in settings where the non-Christian population was present (Acts 2:41; 8:12; 10:48; 16:15, 33). However, baptism in this country has become an in-house rite that witnesses to the faith community of a person's faith in Christ. It is less and less a sign to the world of a person's movement from a secular existence to a God-centered existence. Convenience and culture, nicety and propriety seem to influence us in our practice of baptism. While some still cling to the river or lake baptism as nostalgic remnants of the past, most have built tanks into the church sanctuary where candidates, in a nice and dignified setting, can be conveniently baptized within the structural setting of the people of God.

This shift would not be offensive if it were not for the fact that it represents a change in the direction of our witness. Baptism has been considered an outward sign to the world of what Christ has inwardly accomplished by grace through His indwelling presence making us dead to the world and alive to Christ. Baptismal services in church buildings, observed only by the people of God, do not witness to the world out of which the new believer is stepping. Again, the church abroad instructs the American church by the way they view and practice baptism. Franco Santonocito baptizes six to twelve candidates every year on a public beach near Rome. As he begins to give a clear message concerning the meaning of baptism many curious sunbathers and holiday tourists gather to see what is happening. Each candidate in turn gives his or her testimony and is baptized in the sea, making public declaration of the movement from a life of sin to a life of grace. These public testimonies, with their focus on the witness to God's cleansing power and grace, have resulted in inquiries from those who were among the observing crowd, and some of these have later received Christ as Lord.

In the Church of God at West Anderson our baptistry is located in the narthex. Prior to construction we considered our theology of baptism. Two considerations that prompted us to construct the baptismal area in the narthex were: (1) our belief that baptism is a visible sign or rite celebrating and denoting our entrance into the Church through faith in Christ, so we envisioned the proper place for the baptistry at the entrance of the church; (2) we believe that baptism is a witness to the world apart from Christ to the fact that movement has occurred from the world and its values to Christ and His values, thus the witness should occur not in the sanctuary, apart from the world, but in a place more aligned with the church's meeting and association with the world. When candidates present themselves for baptism they are encouraged to invite their non-Christian friends to the baptism and are instructed carefully about the witness of their baptism in regard to their old life in the world.

In almost every baptismal service in which I have been privileged to participate there have been individuals baptized who are not, strictly speaking, making a direct movement from death to life at that precise point in their life. They desire to communicate another message through their water baptism. These are persons who have previously been baptized, but who have had a dramatic and profound rebirth and desire to be baptized again. Perhaps they have apostatized and desire to meet the Lord in the baptismal waters, recommitting their lives to Christ. They may be somewhat like the disciples in Ephesus who had experienced the baptism of John, but had never really experienced the indwelling of the Spirit of God. Paul suggested that they be baptized in the name of Jesus, placed His hands upon them and they received the Holy Spirit (Acts 19:1–7). Some persons feel the renewal of the Spirit so strongly that they must in some way symbolize the new life that has begun for them. It would seem that such a confession through baptism is within the spirit of biblical baptism, if not within the scope of exact biblical practice.

This exercise of theological reflection upon our experience of baptism, with its attendant consideration of the scriptural passages referring to baptism, has convinced me that the richness of the baptismal experience is never fully grasped by any one person, group, or time. Nor can one individual say for another what should or should not be experienced in baptism's expression of faith and obedience. God's activity in and through the church and its sacred rites remains something we see, but only as a poor reflection, and we are motivated to give ourselves more fully to what we have not completely grasped but know to be the source of our spiritual life in Christ.

The Christian Church (Disciples of Christ)

HOWARD E. SHORT

Distinguished Editor Emeritus
Christian Board of Publication

In the early summer of 1809, Abram Altars, who was not a member of any church, invited a group of Old Light, Seceder, Anti-Burgher Scotch Presbyterians who were somewhat in limbo, to meet in his home in Washington County, Pennsylvania. Thomas Campbell was the leader of the group. He had been there two years and, until recently, was the assigned pastor of churches in the Chartiers Presbytery of the Associate Synod in Philadelphia. At the May meeting of the Synod, he had read a paper explaining his differences with Synod and Presbytery, after which he was suspended permanently. From his side, he withdrew from the authority of the Synod.

The little band of his followers heard him speak in the Altars home on divisions in the church and how to heal them. He concluded with a statement which soon became a dictum of the group: "Where the Scriptures speak, we speak; where the Scriptures are silent, we are silent."[1] As soon as he finished, Andrew Munro stood up and said, "Mr. Campbell, if we adopt that as a basis, then there is an end of infant baptism."

It was a disturbing moment. At this time, Thomas Campbell didn't really believe that speaking where the Scriptures speak would necessarily mean that they had to give up infant baptism. Later, James Foster asked him how he could baptize a child when the Bible does not authorize it. Campbell is said to have replied, "Sir, you are the most intractable person I ever met."

At the Abrams' home, however, he replied to Mr. Munro that "if infant baptism be not found in the Scripture, we can have nothing to do with it."[2]

Thomas Acheson replied to that by saying, "I hope I may never see the day when my heart will renounce that blessed saying of Scripture, 'Suffer little children to come unto me, and forbid them not, for of such is the kingdom of heaven.'" Then he broke into tears and started to leave when the above-mentioned James Foster said, "Mr. Acheson, I would remark that in the portion of Scripture you have quoted there is no reference, whatever, to infant baptism."[3]

I.

On August 17, 1809, the group organized as "The Christian Association of Washington," hoping to be able to remain just that, a fellowship of Christians and not a new denomination. For nearly two years, the matter of baptism remained an open question. On May 4, 1811, the Association became a church, the Brush Run Church. Alexander Campbell, the son of Thomas, had come to the area from County Armagh, Ireland, in 1809 and soon shared his father's views on most subjects, including baptism.

In the meantime, some of those who were charter members of the Brush Run Church understood baptism to relate to church membership. Since they had not been immersed, they questioned whether they should commune or not. Thomas Campbell was not having much difficulty in deciding against infant baptism, or in immersing adults who had never been baptized. But it was another matter to immerse those who had been baptized as infants. "We could not unchurch ourselves now and go out into the world and then turn back again and enter the church merely for the sake of decorum," he said.[4] Nevertheless, Thomas Campbell immersed three adults, July 4, 1811. James Foster didn't approve, and questioned how an unimmersed person could perform the ceremony.

The matter came to a head after the marriage of Alexander Campbell and Margaret Brown, March 11, 1811, and the birth of their first child, one year and two days later. They had to face the decision of whether to have the baby girl baptized or not. The decision was negative, and three months later, June 12, 1812, the young Campbells and a sister of Alexander—and the parents, too, Mr. and Mrs. Thomas Campbell, were immersed in Buffalo Creek. A Baptist minister performed the rite. They made a simple confession that Jesus is the Son of God, and asked to be baptized *"into the name* of the Father, Son and Holy Spirit," not *"in the name* of," as the Baptists were saying. Twenty more were immersed the next Sunday, and soon many more. Those who disagreed withdrew from the Brush Run Church.

When the church was being cited for theological error in 1825 by the Redstone Baptist Association which the church had joined, one error was: "They maintain there is no promise of salvation without baptism; that baptism procures the remission of sins and the gift of the Holy Spirit."[5]

Alexander Campbell wrote in his *Memoirs of Elder Thomas Campbell* that he had asked his father whether his principles would mean giving up infant baptism. This was when Alexander first arrived and he was reading his father's proof sheets of the *Declaration and Address.* "I asked him in what passage . . . we would find a precept or an exact precedent for the baptism or sprinkling of infants. . . . His response, in substance, was, 'It was merely inferential.'"[6]

As the son gradually assumed leadership of the movement, he spoke and wrote more on the subject of baptism. In the *Christian System*, he wrote: "Without previous faith in the blood of Christ, and deep, unfeigned repentance before God, neither immersion in water, nor any other action, can secure to us the blessings of peace and pardon. It can merit nothing. Still to the believing penitent it is the means of receiving a formal, distinct and specific absolution, or release from guilt."[7] This was in 1839.

In a debate with John Walker, which Campbell published under the title, *Infant Sprinkling Proved to Be a Human Tradition*, in 1820, he said: "The outward rite. . . must bear an analogy to the doctrine exhibited in it and by it. Hence, immersion is a beautiful and striking representation of our faith in the death and burial of Christ; and our emerging out of it, a suitable emblem of his resurrection from the grave, and of our obligations to a new life so that the sprinkling of a few drops of water has no analogy to the things signified in baptism."[8]

It was significant to hear Dean Rockwell Harmon Potter say the same thing in a seminary class at Hartford, in 1930. Dr. Potter, at the time, was also president of the American Board of Commissioners for Foreign Missions of the Congregational Church, and had been, for more than twenty years, pastor of Center Church in Hartford. Hence, we were all in awe of him. I did not pose the question, although I may have been the only immersionist in the class. Dean Potter said, "When young couples come to me with their infants for dedication I try to get them to dispense with the water, since a few drops from my fingertips to their children's foreheads is not symbolic of anything—but I always lose!"

Through the years Alexander Campbell felt it necessary to explain further his views on baptism. As editor of the

Christian Baptist from 1823 to 1830, and of the *Millennial Harbinger* from 1831 to his death in 1866, he had ready-made vehicles for his thought, as well as in his published debates and numerous other ways. In 1835 he wrote, "He who has . . . been immersed . . . has only been born into the Kingdom—he has only entered on the race. . . . He has yet to form a Christian character. If he ever wears the crown, he must win it."[9]

For some, immersion was everything. Campbell wrote, in 1840, "That some of my brethren, with too much ardor. . . have given to baptism an undue eminence—a sort of pardon-procuring, rather than a pardon-certifying and enjoying efficacy, I frankly admit; but such has never been my reasonings nor my course."[10] In 1847: "We do not place baptism among good works. . . . In baptism we are passive in everything but in giving our consent. We are buried and raised by another. Hence no view of baptism can be called a good work."[11]

In 1861, Campbell wrote expressing a belief that separated him from numerous others on the subject. "The rehearsal of a 'Christian experience' in order to receive baptism or church fellowship is without. . . precedent in the Christian Scriptures. . . Faith and faith alone in the person, mission, and redemption of the Lord Jesus Christ, is all that the Christian Institution did, or can, legitimately . . . demand of any candidate for baptism."[12]

II.

Walter Scott, a distant cousin of the novelist, came along as a forceful preacher on the Western Reserve, along with Alexander Campbell, in the seven-year period when the Disciple movement was a part of the Mahoning Baptist Association. Scott's writing, in later years, shows him to be an ardent supporter of immersion, and of the necessity for faith and belief, on the part of the candidate.

In the *Protest Unionist*, in 1847, he ridiculed popular concepts of the steps in the saving process: "While we believe the 'Divinity of the Messiah' to be the greatest proposition in our religion and its creed; they dream of all the propositions in the confession of the matter faith; while we say that

1. Faith comes by evidence and nothing else,
2. Repentance from motive, and
3. Baptism for the remission of sins from authority."[13]

Regarding the form of baptism, he wrote in 1860: "In sprinkling, water loses its transitional characteristic and its typical character. By taking away immersion, the Church has been confounded and made one with the world. A drop of water has the properties of the ocean, but it cannot exhibit a transition."[14]

There was no question in Scott's mind as to the order of events. "The command is not to baptize your children: but be yourself baptized for the remission of your sins. The commission is not, he that is baptized and believes, but 'he that believes and is baptized'; accordingly, the apostles, and evangelists, and first ministers of our religion, baptized only those who had previously believed the gospel."[15]

Scott had developed what came to be called "The Five-Finger Exercise" during his preaching on the Reserve: "Faith, Repentance, Baptism, Remission of Sins, Gift of the Holy Spirit." To him, as to most in the later generations, both the doctrines and the order in which they occur are important.

Scott wrote in the *Evangelist*, "Believers alone now form the church . . . . The Son of God died for sin, and has ordained baptism for the immediate pardon of it; therefore no person should be found holding membership in churches founded on the original gospel, but such as have been baptized for the remission of sins."[16]

But the subject has not been firmly settled, from Thomas Campbell's first doubts in 1809, even to the present day. Alexander Campbell had to deal with it on numerous occasions. His straightforward expression in the *Millennial Harbinger* in 1835 brought plenty of letters to the editor. He wrote, "I cannot treat every unimmersed person as a Pagan, inasmuch as their not having been immersed is because they have been sprinkled; and this is often no more than a simple mistake, and not a voluntary renunciation of the Redeemer's institution. If they have thus erred, I would, perhaps, err more in judging them Pagans and in treating them as such than they err simply in mistaking the meaning of the commandment of the Lord."[17]

Two years later the controversy was still raging. The famous "Lunenberg Letter" came to the editor, from "a conscientious sister" (in Virginia), who wrote: "Does the name of Christ or Christian belong to any but those who believe the *gospel*, repent, and are buried by baptism into the death of Christ?" In a lengthy column of reply, Alexander Campbell said, in part: "But who is a Christian? I answer, Every one that believes in his heart that Jesus of Nazareth is the Messiah, the Son of God; repents of his sins, and obeys him in all things according to his measure of knowledge of his will . . . . Should I find a Pedobaptist more intelligent in the Christian Scriptures, more spiritually-minded and more devoted to the Lord than a Baptist, or one immersed on a profession of the ancient faith, I could not hesitate a moment in giving the preference of my heart to him that loveth most. Did I act otherwise, I would be a pure sectarian, a Pharisee among Christians."[18]

III.

Barton Warren Stone led a few congregations out of fellowship with the Lexington Presbytery, Synod of Kentucky, in 1803 and they formed a Presbytery of their own, the Springfield Presbytery. But it was disbanded the following year on the grounds that such organizations were unscriptural.

In the early months, Stone didn't have much to say about baptism, although he was acquainted with immersionists, of course. He considered it a matter of choice.[19] When he finally made a study of the Scriptures on the subject, he decided that the immersion of believers was the divinely ordained manner, and he himself was immersed. He also taught that baptism was "for the remission of sins." As a result, most of the churches which were formed, or moved from Presbyterianism into the Stone movement, practiced immersion exclusively.

However, the churches never excluded the non-immersed from communion. Stone wrote in the *Christian Messenger*: "You (Campbells) debar unimmersed persons from the Lord's Table. In this you are not correctly informed. We invite none, we debar none; because we have no scriptural authority for either. We sit not as inquisitors on the conscience of any man."[20] Stone favored fellowship of the unimmersed and the immersed, making Christian character the test of fellowship. But he preached repentance and immersion.[21]

Space forbids a more extensive development of Stone's concepts and practices, but it must be noted that this movement was well under way before the Campbells left Ireland. On January 1, 1832, there was a kind of union meeting between followers of the two, Campbell and Stone, in Lexington, Kentucky. It was decidedly informal, consisting of a speech or two and some handshaking. However, the union has persisted to this day, and the divisions which have taken place among the Disciples in this century have not been along Campbell and Stone lines. The three denominations, of which the Christian Church (Disciples of Christ) is one, all have aspects of both original movements among their beliefs and practices.

If the Christians and the Reformers, as the groups were usually named, had departed from the Presbyterians, were they not then almost twins with the Baptists? Not exactly. This, too, is a theme that cannot be pursued in the space at our disposal, but enough can be said to indicate that there was a deep theological difference in their concepts of the meaning and purpose of baptism. People outside the two movements mistakenly observed that they all immersed, and thought they were identical in belief.

Baptists at the time required a believer to make a confession of faith and to give personal testimony of experiences which made the confession seem true. Then the congregation voted to receive the candidate, after which came the immersion. The Disciples followed the already-mentioned steps: faith, repentance, (confession) and baptism. There was no vote by the congregation, on the grounds that it was the Lord's Church, and he received penitent believers into it. Furthermore, the Disciples considered baptism one of the steps in the saving process, while the Baptists insisted that baptism was a *sign* of the forgiveness of sins and a regeneration which had already taken place. To non-immersionists, this may sound like semantics. Suffice it to say that the argument has never subsided, albeit it is normally a friendly one in these days.

IV.

The rest of our discussion should be directed toward present-day beliefs and practices. However, perhaps we can link the past to the present with a short comment on the situation at the close of the War Between the States. The Disciples had not divided, chiefly because they had no machinery for doing so. Almost without realizing it, they had drifted toward different approaches to the old watchword: "Where the Scriptures speak, we speak." What might be called a liberal approach to issues as opposed to a conservative or literal approach to Scriptures was not completely identified with one section of the country, but, generally speaking, southern churches became the nucleus of a more conservative approach.

One strong voice was that of Moses E. Lard, one of my early predecessors as professor of church history in what is now Lexington Theological Seminary. He was sure that "the ancient order of things" was being dissipated, especially regarding baptism, for open communion was being ever more widely practiced. Wrote Lard, in his *Quarterly*, in April 1865:[22]

> Let us agree to commune with the sprinkled sects around us, and soon we shall come to recognize them as Christians. Let us agree to recognize them as Christians, and immersion, with its deep significance, is buried in the grave of our folly. Then in one whit will we be no better than others.

Open communion won the day, in spite of Lard. I have never seen anyone refused communion in either of the three denominations that now exist, during my lifetime, with one exception. That was in a small, country Church of Christ where the elders had decided that one of their own members was not worthy to commune.

Isaac Errett, who was to become editor of one of the most influential papers, the *Christian Standard*, when it was begun in 1866, was a voice to be heard in the second generation. He wrote, in 1861,[23] to say that Disciples existed for the purpose of uniting Christians, not to further divide them, so we are not obligated to "unchristianize" those who have not been immersed. He did not believe "close communion" could be justified because there were many devout Christians who had not been immersed. This is the view which has prevailed.

But open communion and open membership are two different matters. The Disciples have not settled this issue. Some will try to be logical. The argument goes this way: Everyone is welcome at the Lord's Table, at the Lord's invitation. Neither the congregation nor leaders of the church as a whole make any attempt to intervene. But every congregation has its rules as to whether a non-immersed Christian can become a member or not. An unknown number of congregations say "Not!" None of these, so far as I know, would say that we are the "only Christians," but we have a position to maintain. We believe immersion is baptism and feel that this view should be perpetuated in the present day. Our witness would be weakened, if we let down the barriers.

At the same time Moses E. Lard was making his exclusive arguments, Lewis L. Pinkerton was advocating open membership, as early as 1869. To do otherwise was to question the character of the "pious unimmersed," he felt.[24] When William T. Moore became minister of a congregation in London, he led the congregation in this practice.

Various churches have been considered the leaders in an open membership policy, with a group around the University of Chicago—Edward Scribner Ames, Herbert L. Willett, Charles Clayton Morrison, and the Baltimore pastor, Peter Ainslie, usually getting the credit—or the blame. However, it is known that the Cedar Avenue Church in Cleveland was open, in 1895, and the Southside Christian Church in Indianapolis a year later.

In 1929, Alfred T. DeGroot, later to become a well-known church history professor at Drake University and at

Texas Christian University, made a study of 8,399 congregations and found only nineteen which openly received the
unimmersed into membership. Eleven years later, DeGroot
wrote that "conversations with large numbers of ministers
since that time has revealed that many of them, probably
some hundreds, employ the practice with or without approving action by their churches, and that at least scores of
churches have adopted open membership, but for the sake of
allaying controversy they give no general publicity to this
policy."[25]

V.

In the 1920s word came back to some of the church
papers that our missionaries were receiving unimmersed
persons into their congregations. For example, a Methodist
came from one Chinese city to another where the Disciples
had a little church. Logically, it would seem the thing to do,
in a land of hundreds of millions of Buddhists and Confu-
cianists, and a very few thousand Christians, to welcome a
fellow-Christian. But someone saw this Methodist serving as
an elder at the Lord's Table. The Missionary Society felt
called upon, at the 1922 International Convention, to
declare that "in harmony with the teachings of the New
Testament (we receive) only those who are immersed, penitent believers in Christ."[26] This might have made matters
worse—if that Methodist served communion, and was not
even a member!

The upshot of this latest confrontation was the organizing of the North American Christian Convention, at a rump
session during the 1926 Memphis meeting of the International Convention. This group developed into the body now
listed in the *Yearbook of American Churches* as "The unde-
nominational fellowship of Christian Churches and
Churches of Christ." To the best of my knowledge the uni-

versal practice in this church is reception of members only by confession of faith and baptism, and if one comes by letter, I believe such a person is asked whether he or she has already been immersed. The number of congregations in this fellowship is roughly the same as those in the Christian Church (Disciples of Christ).

Perhaps the most curious condition in the body to which I belong, to others, is the practice of both closed and open membership. I know of no way to assess the number, or the reasoning behind either practice today. One seldom reads much about it in the papers, or in scholarly studies. While a whole new denomination has developed since 1926, with opposition to open membership as the chief issue at hand, the Christian Church (Disciples of Christ) has restructured itself into some semblance of church order, with the so-called General Manifestation and Regional Manifestations acting as Church. But congregations were not touched, in the Restructure process, and are as free to be mavericks or lambs as they please. The Region and the General Church depend entirely upon the voluntary cooperation of the congregations to carry out their programs. It works surprisingly well. But some congregations will receive any confessing Christian into membership, upon a statement of membership elsewhere. This includes Friends, or others, who may not practice any outward rites of baptism and communion. And other congregations hold to the necessity of confession and immersion for church members.

Thus, I have to leave this short study of the concepts and practices of the Christian Church (Disciples of Christ) in a very untidy shape. I can only generalize from observation as follows: We began to practice believers' baptism, by immersion, because it was considered to be the New Testament practice, and we were going to restore the New Testament Church; we were soon convinced that it was the true and only doctrine for baptism; from the beginning the Stone side of the movement was reluctant to exclude non-immersed persons from the Lord's Table, and Alexander Campbell came to this viewpoint also—so we never believed that we were the "only Christians."

What seemed like mutually exclusive views have been reconciled by perhaps the majority today, so that believers' baptism by immersion is the only belief and practice of the Church, but this view is not forced upon others who find our fellowship appealing but consider their previous baptism, even as infants, to be satisfactory. Ah, logic and faith! Should one's religion make sense? Our Alexander Campbell was a man of reason above all else. But in the long run, "by their fruits you shall know them" may be an even better criterion of one's religion than either ancient or modern creeds.

The Churches of Christ

EARL WEST

Professor of Church History
Harding Graduate School of Religion

Alexander Campbell expressed a viewpoint on believers' baptism in 1828 that generally represents what most members of the Churches of Christ hold to be true. Campbell then stated:

> Immersion in water into the name of the Father, Son and Holy Spirit, the fruit of faith in the subject, is the most singular that ever appeared in the world. Although very common in practice, and trite in theory, although the subject of a good many volumes, and of many conversations, it appears to me that this institution of divine origin, so singular in its nature, and so grand and significant in its design, is understood by comparatively few. In my debate with Mr. MaCalla in Kentucky in 1823, on this topic, I contended that it was a divine institution designed for putting the legitimate subject of it in actual possession of the remission of sins—That to every believing subject it did formally, and in fact convey to him the forgiveness of sins. It was with much hesitation I presented this view of the subject at that time, because of its perfect novelty. I was then assured of its truth, and, I think, presented sufficient evidence of its certainty. But having thought still more closely on the subject, and having been necessarily called to more fully as an

essential part of the Christian religion, I am still better prepared to develop its import and to establish its utility and value in the Christian religion . . . .

He proceeded to compare baptism to the laver which stood between the brazen altar and the sanctuary. In the laver, filled with water, the priests washed themselves before they approached the sanctuary. It was the bath of purification. Christian immersion, he pointed out, stands in relation to the Christian temple as the bath of purification stood in the Jewish—"Between the sacrifice of Christ and acceptable worship." He urged his readers to study Eph. 5:26, Titus 1:5, and Hebrews 10:23.[1]

Later, in the same series of articles Campbell explained, "We connect faith with immersion as essential to forgiveness—and therefore, as was said of old, 'according to your faith, so be it unto you,' so say we of immersion." He added that he that goeth down into the water to put on Christ, in the faith that the blood of Jesus cleans from all sin, and that he has appointed immersion as the medium, and the act of ours, through and in which he actually and formally remits our sins, has, when immersed, the actual remission of sins." So, Campbell summarized it that in baptism one puts on Christ, is buried with him, rises with him, has his sins remitted, enters upon a new life, receives the Holy Spirit, and begins to rejoice in the Lord.[2]

Thus, Campbell expressed a viewpoint that baptism was an immersion in water, that it was the "fruit of faith," that it was performed in the name of the Father, Son, and Holy Spirit, that it was a divine institution, and that it was the door of entrance into the divine Christian temple, the church of Christ. While members of the Churches of Christ feel under no obligation to accept a thing because Campbell said it, they generally agree that his statement is a statement of Scripture.

It would, therefore appear that these statements adequately cover the entire range of baptism in so far as a general statement is concerned. It would also seem evident that among those who share this point of view there would be little room for disagreements. This has hardly been the case. Campbell saw baptism as a part of the "ancient gospel," which was equally a part of the "ancient order of things." As he saw it, the total return to this ancient order was the only route to cure all the ills of religion and to make Christianity totally acceptable to God.

It will be the purpose of this paper to sketch briefly some of the internal problems that arose within the "restoration movement" and later, among the Churches of Christ, that were linked in some way to this explicit conception of baptism.

I.

After his defense of Protestantism against Roman Catholicism in his famous debate with the Cincinnati Bishop Purcell in January 1837, Campbell became less rigid in contending that baptism was the "door of entrance into the Christian temple." The problem thrust itself on him at this time, as to the spiritual status of members of the Protestant bodies. If baptism led one into the kingdom of God, and that baptism was an immersion in the name of the Father, Son, and the Holy Spirit, were those who belonged to Protestant bodies who had not submitted to baptism truly Christians? In the famous Lunenberg letter which he received from an anonymous Christian lady in Lunenberg, Virginia, he was asked if there were Christians in Protestant bodies. He responded,

> In reply to this conscientious sister, I observe, that if there be no Christians in the Protestant sects, there are

certainly none among the Romanists, none among the Jews, Turks, Pagans, and therefore, no Christians in the world except ourselves, or such of us as keep, or strive to keep, all the commandments of Jesus. Therefore for many centuries there has been no church of Christ, no Christians in the world; and the provisions concerning the everlasting kingdom of Messiah have failed, and the gates of Hell have prevailed against the church! This cannot be; and therefore, there are Christians among the sects.[3]

Campbell also recognized a semantic problem: "But who is a Christian?" His reply was: "I answer, everyone that believes in his heart that Jesus of Nazareth is the Messiah, the son of God; repents of his sins and obeys him in all things according to his measure of knowledge of His will." He added, "I cannot, therefore make any one duty the standard of Christian state or character, not even immersion."

To quote Campbell of 1828 and again of 1837 on baptism appears to be quoting two different people. Yet, the shift in his viewpoint is not as dramatic as it would appear. By June of 1829 Campbell was writing in the *Christian Baptist* that immersion was necessary to get into the "kingdom of favor" (the church), but not into the "kingdom of glory" (heaven). He also now noted that the remission of sins had nothing to do with salvation; instead, salvation was achieved by good works. At the same time he stated, "all who obey . . . according to their knowledge, I am of the opinion will be introduced into that kingdom." Many years later John F. Rowe, who succeeded Benjamin Franklin as editor of the *American Christian Review* expressed the viewpoint that it was Campbell's carrying the banner against Bishop Purcell which caused him to make concessions to Protestantism which did not express what he really believed.[4] This, however, overlooks that viewpoint he expressed between 1829 and 1837 making the same "concessions."

The term Christian admittedly has remained a term with certainly flexible connotations if we consider the general viewpoint. The word implies a certain type of character who possesses holiness of life, integrity, and godly devoutness, among other things. If this is the sum-total of elements to be considered, it would, of course, follow that there are Christians in all religious bodies. In a similar way, these qualities of upright character were also found, though not frequently, in pagan Roman society, so the early church existed side by side with pagans, many of whom lived spiritually admirable lives. But, if one goes a step further and follows the lead of Campbell's 1828 expressions, if baptism secures the remission of sins and gains for one the entrance into the new life and the kingdom of God, then baptism was essential to being a Christian, to being a member of the "Christian temple." There was established, then, an area of conflict in the movement to restore New Testament Christianity.

In the period between 1837 and the Civil War, however, the viewpoint Campbell expressed in the Lunenberg letter received very little attention. The Christian brotherhood faced a rising crescendo of controversy over slavery. Too, the formation of several societies—Missionary, Bible, and Publication—came along with some controversy. Furthermore, Campbell's energies now became more centered in the establishment of Bethany College and seeing it settled on a firm basis so as to guarantee its continuance long after his death. However, the question of whether there were Christians in Protestant bodies arose again during the early days of the Civil War in a controversy that possessed a certain volatility.

A renewal of the conflict over whether or not there were "Christians among the Sects" as it was usually called, stemmed from David King, who, after 1861, was editor of the *British Millennial Harbinger*. King was deeply conservative in all his theological viewpoints, and the Churches of Christ in England were at this time much more conservative than their counterparts in the United States. The dispute passed over to America and to the *Millennial Harbinger*. James T. Walsh, former editor of the *Christian Messenger*, later renamed the *British Millennial Harbinger*, was a close friend of Alexander Campbell. When David King watched a more liberal theological point of view slowly taking over in America, his sympathies turned to Ben Franklin, conservative editor of the *American Christian Review*. In a few months it was evident that W. K. Pendleton, W. T. Moore and Isaac Errett advocated a more liberal position against both David King and Ben Franklin. In declaring there were Christians among the "sects," Pendleton said, ". . . to plead for union and at the same time exclude the really pious from the communion of the body and blood of the Savior, is in the very nature of things to destroy the practical power of our plea . . ." Later, with unsurpassed eloquence Pendleton wrote,

> Will anyone take the absurd position that the noble list of illustrious men, who have been the light and ornament of religion in the ages that are past and whose piety and learning are still the admiration and glory of the Lord's people—that all of these, because of an error, not in the significancy or divine authority of baptism, but what we must be allowed to call it mode—that all these, because of such an error, must be pushed from our ranks as reprobate—torn from our Christian affections as heretics—thrust from the communion of the body and blood of the Savior whom for a long life they so truly loved and so devoutly served, and counted no more worthy of our Christian fellow-

ship than so many heathen and publicans! The conclusion is too monstrous for any but the hide-bound
zealot of a cold and lifeless formalism . . .

Robert Richardson, Campbell's friend, co-teacher, medical
doctor and later his biographer, stated at the same time that
there were Christians among the sects, but not in the full
New Testament usage of the term, but they are "imperfect,"
"embryo," Christians.[5]

By the end of the Civil War, it was evident to most of the
church's leadership that two broad elements had emerged in
this movement to restore the ancient order of things and
these were slowly moving in the opposite directions. The
conservative element was led by the *American Christian
Review* and Elder Ben Franklin while the more liberal one
was led by Isaac Erret in the *Christian Standard* which began
publication April 15, 1866. Too, the *Gospel Advocate* re-
appeared in January 1866, as the *British Millennial Harbinger* noted, to be the voice for southern Christians who advocated a return to the ancient order. However, the passing of
twenty-five years witnessed slow changes in the entire
facade. The conservatism of the *Review*, which was published beginning in 1864 in Anderson, Indiana, intensified,
a trend that continued for many years after the death of its
editor in 1878. As for the *Standard*, it refused advance further
into liberalism despite pressure upon Errett by his good
friend, Senator James A. Garfield and the growing popular-
ity of biblical criticism stemming from German theological
institutions. At the same time, the *Gospel Advocate* remained theologically conservative and, although it flirted
with ultra-conservative viewpoints briefly, it refused to follow in the track of the *Review*. In the century between 1875
and 1975 the *Review* passed from the hands of Franklin, to
John F. Rowe and on to Daniel Sommer, who died in 1940.

The *Review's* influence was powerful in the Midwest and sections of Missouri at the beginning of the twentieth century, but ultimately its extremes proved its undoing. The journal is no longer published and scarcely a handful of people scattered over the nation hold to the old viewpoints. On the other hand, the *Advocate* grew and extended its influence over the nation and into many areas of foreign mission work and remains today the most powerful journal among Churches of Christ the worldover.

This overview, it is hoped, will provide the backdrop for noting the sporadic return of some difference of viewpoint over baptism among conservative Churches of Christ. While agreed that valid baptism was an immersion in water of the believer for the remission of sins, it now became a matter of some discussion whether the believer had to understand at the time of his baptism that he was being immersed for the remission of his sins. The problem at this point had nothing to do with those taught within the Churches of Christ, but referred to those entering the church via baptism which had been administered under the teaching of the Southern Baptists. It was generally understood by Churches of Christ that Baptists taught that remission of sins was granted when one became a believer and that immersion followed as a visible symbol of a divine grace that had previously been bestowed. Although this was not a major element of disagreement, it did appear and each point of view had vigorous adherents.

It was, of course, inevitable that the spotlight would be focused upon Alexander Campbell, who was baptized June 12, 1812 with his wife, father, mother, and sister, Dorothea, "into the Christian faith" by Elder Mathias Luce, a Baptist minister. The question then was, did Campbell understand at the time he was immersed that he was being baptized for the remission of his sins? While on a tour through Virginia in the spring of 1856, Campbell recalled the circumstances that led up to his baptism. His parents had him, as a youth, memorize much of the writings of Paul, especially Romans and Hebrews. "These were my systematic theology, or, rather, my doctrinal christology, to which I owed more than to all my memorizings of the creeds and catechisms of the present Sabbath orthodoxy," he explained. He remembered that baptism was first thrust on his attention following a discourse on "metaphysical creeds and speculative dogmas." After asserting that these were not found in the Scripture, and that nothing but what could be sustained by a 'Thus saith the Lord' should ever be regarded as an article of Christian faith or practice, a friend then replied, "Then, sir, you must become a Baptist; for you cannot find one 'thus said the Lord' for infant baptism, nor an express precedent." Campbell contended that he could do so, but after examining the Scriptures, he repudiated infant baptism."[6]

Campbell was pursuing the course he had resolved upon in 1809 when he arrived in America, and that was to be an "independent" in religion—to examine the Bible for himself and to permit no ecclesiasticism to determine for him what constituted divine truth. The path of independency, however, was not an untroubled one, as he explained a few years later.

> In conformity to the grand principle which I call the polestar of my course of religious inquiry, I was led to question the claims of infant sprinkling to divine authority, and was, after a long, serious and prayerful examination of all means of information, led to solicit immersion on a profession of my faith, when as yet I scarcely knew a Baptist from Washington to Ohio, in the immediate region of my labors, and when I did not know that any friend or relative on earth would concur with me, I was accordingly baptized by Elder

Mathias Luce, who was accompanied by Elder Henry Spears, on the 12th day of June, 1812. In the meantime, I pursued the avocation of a husbandman as a means of my subsistence; and while I discharged, as far as in me lay, the duties of a bishop (having been regularly ordained one of the elders of the church of Christ at Brush Run) and itinerated frequently through the circumjacent country, I did it without any earthly remuneration. I did not at first contemplate forming any connection with the Regular Baptist Association called the 'Redstone' as the perfect independency of the church and the pernicious tendency of human creeds and terms of communion were subjects to me of great concern. As a mere spectator, I did, however, visit the Redstone Association in the fall of 1812. After a more particular acquaintance with some of the members and ministers of that connection, the church of Brush Run did formally agree to unite with that association on the grounds that no terms of union or communion other than the Holy Scriptures should be required. On this ground, after presenting a written declaration of our belief (always distinguishing betwixt making a declaration of our faith for the satisfaction of others and binding that declaration on others as a term of commmunion), we united with the Redstone Association in the fall of 1812 in which connection the church of Brush Run yet continues . . . . [7]

The discussion over what exactly Campbell did understand at the time of his baptism was fed by certain ambiguities in his statements. His widow, however, sought a certain clarity late in her life, and explained:

Some of the brethren thought that because remission of sins' was not named at his baptism, he was not scripturally introduced into Christ's kingdom. Alexander Campbell was baptized in the full faith of the forgiveness of his sins, when baptized into Christ's death and a full hope of the resurrection unto eternal life; having been planted in Christ in the likeness of his death, that he was assured he would participate in his resurrection, and this burial and resurrection imply a death unto him and an enjoyment of a new life in Christ, no longer living a servant of sin, nor yielding his members to serve sin. Of course, he was freed from the guilt and pollution of sins, and fully enjoyed a new life, with the pardon of all his past sins, for the promise was to him.[8]

II.

The question, however, of what Campbell understood at the time of his baptism is only an academic one so it emerged infrequently as a topic of discussion. The question of receiving those into the church who had been immersed under the teaching of Baptist theology came to be more heated and longer lasting in the differences between two men—David Lipscomb and Austin McGary—and two papers—the *Gospel Advocate* and the *Firm Foundation*. McGary, an outspoken and often bitter Civil War veteran, was one of the hardy pioneers bred on the frontier of Texas who understood only how to be rough and vigorous and seldom gentle or kind. He was almost obsessed with the viewpoint that converts to the Churches of Christ coming from the Baptists must be re-baptized because they were baptized to show they had already received remission of sins and not in order to receive it. David Lipscomb, on the other hand, was slightly less rigid. Reared among the Baptists in the lower part of middle Tennessee, Lipscomb's father had been led out of the Baptist church by his reading the *Christian Baptist.* David and his brother, William, attended school under Tolbert Fanning at Franklin College and from Fanning learned a certain independence of thought. In one of his early preaching experiences, a woman responded to the invitation. She explained she had formerly been a Baptist and that here, she had been immersed. David asked her why she had done this, and she replied, "to obey God." Lipscomb brooded over the incident for much of his life. He stated that he could not improve on her answer at the time and after years of reflection, he was yet unable to do so.

So firmly did Austin McGary believe that Lipscomb was in error, that he founded the *Firm Foundation* in Austin, Texas in 1884 to combat Lipscomb's heresy. While Lipscomb never doubted that baptism was for the remission of sins, he contended that this limited the purpose of baptism much too far. Baptism brought one into the symbolic union of Christ's death and resurrection, it was the fruit of faith, it was the door of entrance into the kingdom of God aside from its being an expression of obedience to the commands of God. For thirty years the controversy sporadically rocked both papers and provided a certain type of entertainment to readers. When the controversy ceased, it was because both men were getting old and the readers had grown weary.

What impact have these controversies had on the Churches of Christ in this day? It is unlikely that many members know they ever occurred. Some of the more studious preachers are aware of these background conflicts. Occasionally, they resurface at some college lectureship where vigorous proponents state a position and feelings may run high for the moment. Still, these controversies are not on-going affairs.

Modern problems in a turbulent American society currently receive much more attention. The prevalence of divorce in the 1970s has caused attention to be directed to the Christian home and scarcely a lectureship is conducted in any Christian college but that skillful women teachers speak to other women on some vital aspect of the home and its Christian elements. Concomitant with this is a growing emphasis on counselling and the number of young preachers graduating from Christian schools with a major in counselling is beginning to surpass the majors in Bible. There are numerous workshops developing skills in evangelism and others in developing leadership for local churches that occupy much of the attention in Churches of Christ today.

Preaching the gospel remains the central focus of the Churches of Christ though in a few larger, wealthy congregations down in Texas, the preacher appears to many to occupy a role like a corporation executive—overlooking the activities of a well-organized constituency.

Still, all the basics are there. Churches of Christ take pride in operating by the Bible which all, except a small minority, still hold to be the inspired word of God. Membership still continues to be those who are believers, who, on that faith were immersed for the remission of their sins, so all came into the church purified from sin. Their spiritual development, however, has not always been uniform. Each congregation consists of those who are supremely spiritual people and who enjoy a close walk with God, while others lag behind and are spiritually underdeveloped and totally negative. But this is not unique with any people who try to be religious in a world where religious values are widely considered of dubious value.

The Friends

HUGH BARBOUR

Professor of Religion
Earlham College

It is important to speak first of Quaker worship, to make clear the meaning of Quaker ideas about ministry and sacraments. In this gathering, I need to make clear also the difference between early Quakers and modern ones, in all their variety, though their common roots remain. And I will stress the uniquely Quaker outlooks, rather than the Evangelical beliefs which most Quakers, especially Evangelical Friends, share with other Christians. I need also to describe not just the depth of Quaker silence in worship, but the relationship to Protestants' experience and doctrine about worshipping together before God.

Quakers learned from Luther that God not only gave us in Jesus his own Word of forgiveness, but that in the same way, "we may all be priests," and indeed "may all be Christs to one another."[1] Thus *all ministry by any person may be sacramental.* But Quakers also witness that the work of God's Spirit in our human worshipping, and in human speaking in ministry, cannot be determined by fixed or outward forms. This other message we have also from Luther: the risk is idolatry, confusing human acts with God's. It was applied by the Anabaptists and Pietists, more carefully than by Luther himself, to all Church establishments, showing the need for toleration. But it was applied by the early Quakers to the sacraments and ministry itself. We may return later to any problems this suggests about a dualism of the spiritual versus the physical realities, or about "the inward and the outward man" as Luther called them.[2] The Quaker "Children of the Light" simply affirm that the issue is *human versus divine initiative.* Early Quaker preachers constantly gave prophetic warnings against *"will-worship,"* against any prayer or message spoken, any Psalm or hymn sung, or even any inward praying, that did not come directly for that occasion from the Spirit within those present.

This gives a clearer meaning to Quaker silence. Robert Barclay wrote in his *Apology:*

> As our worship consisteth not in words, so neither in silence, as silence; but in a holy dependence of the mind upon God . . . The Spirit of God should be the immediate actor, mover, persuader and influencer of man in the particular acts of worship; . . . Everyone is thus gathered, and so met inwardly in their spirits, as well as outwardly in their persons; there the secret power and virtue of life is known to refresh the soul, and the pure motions . . . of God's Spirit arise, . . . which edifies the church. And no man here . . . limits the Spirit of God, nor bringeth forth his own conned and gathered stuff . . . Yea, though there be not a word spoken, yet is the true spiritual worship performed, . . . our souls have been greatly edified and refreshed, and our hearts wonderfully overcome with the secret sense of God's power and Spirit, which without words hath been ministered from one vessel to another.[3]

This approach calls to mind Augustine, Julian of Norwich's prayer to God as "the ground of our beseeching," and Thomas Kelly's sense of being "prayed through" in "infused prayer that flows through us into the world of men" so that "we are impelled to pray for particular persons or particular situations with a quiet or turbulent energy that . . . seems utterly irresistible."[4]

Along with a sense of God's initiative, the objectivity of the group character of the Quaker experience of worship provides for Friends the check to subjectivity which in other branches of Christianity is provided by the continuity of sacred tradition. This is our form of knowing which we share in a process no individual could achieve alone, as when Whittier left the clamor of nature,

> And from the silence multiplied,
> by these still forms on either side
> The world that time and sense have known,
> falls off and leaves us God alone.[5]

Some of this sharing may be psychological; to use the quotation Friends love to take from Barclay,

> . . . as many candles lighted, and put in one place, do greatly augment the light, and make it to shine forth, so when many are gathered together into the same life, there is more of the glory of God, and his power appears, to the refreshment of each individual: for that he partakes not only of the light and life raised in himself, but in all the rest.[6]

The experience might be emotionally very intense, as early Friends felt what seemed to be the power of the Spirit shaking their bodies in a physical way:

> Sometimes the power of God will break forth into a whole meeting, and there will be such an inward

> travail, while each is seeking to overcome the evil in
> themselves, that . . . trembling and a motion of body
> will be upon most, if not upon all, which as the power
> of truth prevails will from pangs and groans and with
> a sweet sound of thanksgiving and praise.

From such moments Friends got their nickname of Quakers. They differed, however, from groups with similar behavior, such as "Holy Rollers," in the degree to which "power" was shaped by "truth," and the fearful experience of insight into the "spiritual states" of individuals was awareness of one's personal failings in detail, under the inner searchlight which Friends called "the witness of God in every man." The "Light within," as early Friends embodied it, was no candle of the Lord made of men's invincible spirits, but the Spirit of Christ himself as judge and guide.

The shared nature of Quaker experience thus applied even more to Truth than to emotions. Truth is objective over against our own desires, because it is universal, capable of being seen by all. The true inner theological dialogue in Protestantism, parallel to Roman Catholics' about sacraments, is expressed in terms of the meaning of the *Word* of God. Now Quakers have as central and sacramental sense of Truth and Word as any Protestant. Hence we too have biblical *literalists,* Evangelical Friends for whom the textual *Words* of the Bible are the ultimate authority; for our liberals words are human and symbolic, and the work of the Spirit through words is as much a mystery as the incarnation in Jesus.

But, reflecting our shared experience with the Believers' Churches, we also know the Word of God to be *personal* as much as *universal,* personal in its source, but also personal in its impact upon ourselves, in its *testing* and *overturning* of our own identities: ethical in judgment and command, also ethical in the deeper sense of changing who we are.

Along with awareness of the universal or common nature of the truth they shared, Friends thus sensed behind the ethical power a common personal presence: the ethical Puritan God:

> They come to find the good arise over the evil, and the pure over the impure, in which God reveals himself, and draweth near to every individual, and . . . is in the midst in the whole body, . . . whereby each is a sharer in the whole body, as being a living member of the body, having a joint fellowship and communion with all.[7]

Like Robert Barclay, Isaac Penington early used the language of sacraments in describing the Quaker meetings for worship.

> For we own the blood of the Lord Jesus Christ both outwardly and inwardly, both as it was shed on the Cross, and as it is sprinkled in our consciences.[8]

In this less flesh-despising century, when Friends do not, like Elias Hicks, despise the hemoglobin of Jesus, many Quakers have written to claim that for us all of life and every meal is sacramental.[9] But this seems true only in the sense that Catholics make holy water and incense into "sacramentals." With Lutherans we like to say that "the real presence" is also sensed in our communion. But a closer link to the meaning of the Mass is the Quaker awareness that the worshipping group is itself become "the body of Christ" in which the outward and physical is transformed by the shared Spirit. Alan Kolp, Dean of our Earlham School of Religion, and an Athanasian scholar out of Harvard, likes to lecture on *Friends, Sacraments and Sacramental Living*[10] naturally using John 15:15, the text about Friends:

> Jesus, as God's Son, is ready to step into history with a ministry that can be called sacramental. He does not "do" sacraments; he *is* sacramental . . . He is to be uniquely God's visible sign of God's invisible but real presence. . . . This reality can also be represented through . . . a community of his friends gathered in his name. . . . The gathered meeting for worship may finally be the most effective and powerful sign to communicate that transforming reality which was Jesus.

Nevertheless, for early Friends, the transformation was also a response to real commands of God within, and specific human needs and truth; and those who call themselves "Catholic Quakers" today sound to us more like Anabaptists.

This brings forward the meaning of ministry among Friends. We should first distinguish *ministry within Quaker worship* and *prophetic witness to outsiders*, even though both are assumed to be directly prompted by God's spirit. What a Quaker says during worship, particularly if it is spoken prayer, is said *for* quite as much as *to* the whole group. We can call it *sacramental ministry* in the same double sense that in the Eucharist the elements are offered first obediently to God, and then shared by the whole congregation. Even the impulse to speak may come to more than one person: I can add my own to the many stories of someone in Quaker meeting feeling led to give a message or prayer, which another Friend present then unexpectedly delivers. Supposedly the Friend who speaks turns later to the one still sitting in silence, and adds "next time, say it thyself."

The power of some of these messages may be unexpected to the sharer of what seemed a purely private vision or experience. At other times, strengthening others or giving counsel is consciously intended. John Banks, a Cumberland farm boy who became a Quaker in 1654, reported the first day he attended a Quaker meeting:

> The Lord's power in the Meeting so seized upon me that I was made to cry out in the bitterness of my Soul, in a true sight and sense of my Sins, . . . and the same Day at Evening, as I was going to a Meeting, . . . by the way I was smitten to the ground with the weight of God's judgment for Sin, . . . and I was taken up by two Friends . . . . So a Friend being touched with a sense of my Condition, was made willing to read a Paper in the Meeting (there being but a very few Words spoken) which was suitable to my condition.[11]

Our pastoral Friends in "programed" Quaker church services take much comfort from the fact that even early Friends sometimes felt led to use a previously prepared script.

At other times, however a *prophetic message* to people still closed against the Light was forced upon the early Quaker: Banks himself reported that a few months later,

> . . . as I was sitting in Silence waiting upon the Lord, in a Meeting of Friends upon Pardshaw-Cragg, a weighty Exercise fell upon my Spirit, and it opened in me That, I must go to the Steeple-House in Cockermouth, which was hard for me to give up to; But the Lord by his Power made me to shake and tremble, and by it I was made willing to go. But I would have known what I might do there, which was the cause that for a little time I was . . . darkened. . . . And as I

was going, it appeared to me as if the Priest [of the Cockermouth parish church] had been before me; and it opened in me [to say] "If thou be a Minister of Christ, stand to prove thy practice, and if it be the same the Apostles and Ministers of Christ was, I'll own thee; but if not, I am sent of God this Day to testifie against thee.[12]

Banks went, and he spoke as it had been opened to him. The "hireling priest," George Larcom, "cried out, 'There is one come into the church like a madman with his hat on his head. Church wardens, put him out.' The people were in a great uproar, some to beat me, and some to save me from being beat," and Banks "came away in sweet peace." Whatever levels of his own mind contributed to Banks' impulse to minister, he clearly went to Cockermouth neither out of conscious desire to help the priest nor as a mission outreach from his Quaker meeting, but simply to obey direct calls from God.

Such a sudden call to a single act of ministry, whether prophetic or within the Quaker worship, might happen to any Quaker man or woman of any social or educational background. We celebrate Mary Fisher's call to preach to the Sultan of Turkey and Mary Dyer's to lay down her life as protest against Puritanism in Massachusetts. At any time a Friend might feel led to speak in worship, and if the call was sat on, might share with older Friends his uncertainty. When lengthy services of counseling or physical aid were needed, Friends were taught by George Fox himself to appoint Elders and Overseers, and to divide into Men's and Women's Monthly Meetings for Business. I could have taken more time here to describe the Quaker process of individual discussion by prospective members with Elders and Overseers, testing their readiness for membership. Overseers also

guide conduct, and Elders encourage and restrain those who
speak in meetings for worship. The history of Eldership has
been much studied by Quakers lately. These are the roles we
now consider pastoral: but ministry is for everyone. Social
custom soon pressed men and wealthier Friends into taking
on the services needing expensive travel, as had not been true
at first. At times a local Meeting or national General Meeting would feel responsible to raise money in support of a
member who had felt called to a distant mission, or else to
support his family at home. This again has given comfort to
pasteurized Quaker ministers nowadays; but classically
there was never a salary except for school teachers, nor was
money provided by those to whom a Quaker preached. The
change to salaried pastors came in Meetings in Iowa, Ohio,
and Indiana from the 1870s through 1910, wherever close
contacts with "holiness churches" made annual revivals and
frequent conversions of outsiders a normal part of their
worship. Quaker evangelists often began with "Union Revivals" of several denominations or in "Holiness Bible
Camps" and settled into a single Meeting to continue as
pastors. Their role in calling people to God's power within
them gradually merged into exhortation, though prayer and
the selection of Scriptures and hymns still come spontane-
ously from any member of these "Evangelical Friends
Churches." It may be the *form* of their worship that is
"programed," not its *content*. The silent worship pattern
remains dominant, however, among English and all European Quakers, in the older Meetings of the American east
coast and the newer ones in big cities and college towns.
There it is natural that if anyone there speaks "in ministry"

> since the vocal message is followed by silence, oppor-
> tunity is given for the hearers to carry it further for
> themselves, and the highest vocal exercise is spoken
> prayer.

> This Spirit is limited in its operations by setting up a particular man or men to preach and pray in man's will, . . . and all the rest are excluded . . . and are led merely to depend upon the preacher, . . . and come not thither to meet with the Lord, and to wait for the inward motions of his Spirit.[13]

When Friends have responded to the sacraments, therefore, it has often been the result of immediate impulse, as when David Updegraff, the evangelical Quaker revivalist, visiting in a Baptist friend's church, suddenly felt led to ask for immersion. With equal inconsistency, some of us will share in Communion when we are part of a group of Christians or even of our own wider families, where the sacrament expresses the common worship of a community in which we share. Friends are also aware of 1900 years of Christian history in which some forms of the sacraments have been accepted by almost all Christians. In ecumenical gatherings we may insist on nothing more than the non-necessity of sacraments for salvation, which in light of Catholics' baptism of desire and baptism of blood may not be as rare a doctrine as we imagine. But what such gestures really do is to reduce the sacraments to outwardly casual signs of an inwardly essential spirit, undefined.

Of the specific sacraments, since our Penance is Priestless, the most orthodox is marriage; here all Christian tradition affirms that the *Word* of the betrothed couple is the medium of the Sacrament, and the blessing of the witnesses sharing the event is vital but not priestly, while ethical intention at the level of one's central identity opens the way for the power of God.

About baptism, therefore, Quakers have from the beginning insisted that the true Water of Life was baptism inwardly by purification by the Spirit. This is not considered to happen either suddenly or once for all, except by a few Evangelical Friends. William Penn and George Fox usually equated it with the inner purging we found John Banks going through. In a running debate with Baptists and Anglicans from 1653 into the eighteenth century, Friends naturally recruited Baptist allies in attacking the sprinkling of infants: Even the "great commission" in Matthew's gospel spoke of "teaching all nations" just as it commended baptizing them, and simultaneously making them disciples:

> . . . infants not being capable of teaching, so are not capable of being made Disciples.[14]

The water baptism of adults, which admittedly John the Baptist practiced with Jesus' approval, was interpreted by Friends, on the other hand, as a "type" or "figure"[15] no more permanent than circumcision, which Friends assume that Jesus indulged on account of human weakness, just as Paul so evidently did in 1 Corinthians 1:14. John the Baptist himself could be quoted on the superiority of baptism with the Spirit and with fire. Whether the issue was Calvinist predestination, which Quakers rejected almost blindly, or the purification from sin by outward water, Friends at all periods have carried the baptism issue as a challenge to other churches: Why is it needed?

The Eucharist has been a harder issue for Friends, despite the underlying disagreements once again among other Christians too. Again, Quaker dualists tended to set the letter against the spirit, the outward form against the inward substance, which it was assumed Friends shared as Christ's real presence in our worship. The inward eating of flesh, which Christ demands in John's Feeding of the Multitudes passage, not at the Last Supper,[16] was clearly, said Barclay, identical with the Light and Life of Christ, which were essential but not physical.[17]

Once again this separation of the physical and spiritual by early Friends may seem troublesome. After all, George Fox so stressed the spirituality of Jesus' resurrection body, located everywhere in the universe, not on a throne in a physical heaven, that consequently Fox took more literally than we realize the actual taking in of the risen Christ into ourselves in worship. Just when we are tempted to accept attacks by scholars like Melvin Endy, however, who insist that Quakers were Platonic dualists at heart like Penn's friend Henry More, we remind ourselves that both the Quakers and Puritans made the physical and the spiritual one in ethics. The Quakers' bugbear was always the Catholic sacraments as human manipulations of God, also as fixed forms independent of God's control. Barclay and others did not condemn the sacraments of those weaker in faith than the Quakers, any more than Paul condemned those too weak to eat meat offered to idols. There lurks in the background of Barclay's approach, if not in Fox's, an idea not too distant from Luther's doctrine of receiving sacraments by faith. Hence our temptation to ask once again only, "Is it necessary?"

But once again, Quakers in the effort to spiritualize or make casual the physical element in other people's Eucharists, stressing the memorial or community aspects of the Supper, may be in danger of losing sight of our own witness. Worship is serious business. If God makes it relative to the time, the person, or the community in some degree, he does not thereby give us the right to make it optional, a matter of preference. Quakers do speak out of the silence about the sunlight on the trees or the problems of politics. We are as tempted as anyone else to focus on the mediating processes through which we encounter God; the casual meditations of Quakers may be shallower than any sacrament could be, or again better only because less binding. Perhaps the stark nakedness of worship in Quaker silence is needed to remind us that in worship we meet no culture product or artistic achievement; we meet no one but God. Do we commit a mortal sin by *not* asking as the sacramentalists do, whether God has chosen his own unique channels of mediation? Quakers seem to be the ultimate Protestants, since we try to set aside every mediation except Jesus, and set aside even dogmas about him, the images of Christ by which we make him too after our own image. At times this calls us to say a flat "No!" to outward sacraments; at others we are called to learn from the means of grace others have been given.

SECTION II:
"Baptism, Eucharist, and Ministry": Its Origin, Interpretation, and Application

An Appreciative Testimony Concerning the Baptism of Infants

LOUIS WEEKS

Dean
Louisville Presbyterian Seminary

I am pleased indeed to share with you study of the text entitled "Baptism, Eucharist, and Ministry," (B.E.M.)[1] drafted by the Faith and Order Commission of the World Council of Churches. I personally hope the communion that forms the branch of the Protestant limb of the Christian tree to which I belong—the Presbyterian Church (USA)—will endorse thoroughly the sentiments and doctrine shared therein. I am confident that Lewis Mudge, who helped form the document and who receives profound respect throughout our communion, will be able with others to lead the PCUSA toward endorsement of B.E.M.

I hope likewise that the Churches in which you participate will give thorough study and appropriate approval as well. It is for that reason I am willing to come joyfully into this lion's den of believers' baptism in order to defend the practice and theology of infant baptism. Believe me, I am neither a professor of liturgics nor the offspring of a liturgical professional. The mainstay of my own research is the mere history of American religious experience. When I told a colleague I would be defending pedobaptism amid this august body, she said, "Keep the motor running in your car. You will surely need a quick escape route!

No, I am not a ready controversialist. I read of one—for Nathan Rice debated Alexander Campbell and defended infant baptism to entertain midwesterners (if not to edify them) during November/December, 1843.[2] Rice evidently loved the competitive fray. He evidently let a vivid imagination run away with him, too, for a Catholic priest in Bardstown, Kentucky won a libel suit against him in the early 1840s. Such activities may have provided partisan sport, but they failed to witness to unity in Christ, to oneness in the Holy Spirit, or to the one who made us all.

On the contrary, what brings me here is the conviction that we are one in Christ Jesus our Lord. I believe that we participate in one Church in which Christ is head. This effort on "Baptism, Eucharist, and Ministry" seems to be a constructive attempt to allow various portions of the Body of Christ to rejoice in the potential health and coordination of the many members.

This B.E.M. document is so good that I am tempted merely to read forty minutes worth of it to you. Note, for example, the first paragraph on "The Institution of Baptism." Notice the document begins with the gospel, the good news of Christ's death and resurrection. Note how fully it uses the Bible. Note the emphasis on God's grace, the beginning, and the current life of Christians in all times and places. Notice the willingness to speak of God's "New Covenant" with God's people.

Notice how the meaning of baptism receives careful attention before the varieties within Christian practice become focal ones. All of the kinds of meaning mentioned— "Participation in Christ's Death and Resurrection," "Conversion, Pardoning, and Cleansing," "The Gift of the Spirit," "Incorporation into the Body of Christ," and "The Sign of the Kingdom"—all are vital in all the Christian traditions, melding emphases of Eastern and Western limbs, of Catholic and Protestant branches, and of the various churches within each part of the whole.

I honestly think the treatment of believers' baptism in the sections on "Baptism and Faith" and "Baptismal Practice" are excellent portrayals of that vital indispensable tradition. I, who advocate and am nourished spiritually by sharing in the baptism of infants, can understand and participate in the power of believers' baptism as set forth in B.E.M. I trust a reciprocal process of sharing can be engaged from Christians who find sustenance through believers' baptism.

I grant the difficulty in reciprocation. Mennonites, Puritan Baptists, and subsequent, related Christian bodies have found some identity in self-definition over against pedobaptists. And I will grant that believers' baptism may prevail (for what that personal concession is worth). Easter Sunday in the congregation where I normally worship, four of the nine members of the confirmation class were also baptized (as all nine made profession). Next year a majority? Perhaps. The PCUSA has moved explicitly to honor believers' baptism in its *Book of Order* for the forming denomination. But even if we Presbyterians come to see the light and foreswear our pedobaptist foolishness, doubtless a Christian majority will continue among Orthodox and Roman Catholic, Lutheran, Reformed, and Anglican bodies to whom all of us Presbyterians, Baptists, and Anabaptist-derived denominations are numerically small potatoes.

To mention the congregation in which I worship is to broach the heart of my testimony in behalf of infant baptism. For me, and for most others in the congregation, no other moment exceeds in importance that in which a child is received into the visible Body of Christ. I find my heart and soul full of praise and dedication frequently in worship. The occasion of infant baptism inevitably evokes a full measure of those thoughts and sentiments. Typically, family and friends, children and grownups, really concentrate on the event whenever it occurs. Let me recount just one specific instance in our congregation, an example upon which to draw subsequently.

She did not cry when her parents stood with her in front of the congregation. Sarah Kelton, at two months, simply looked around and took it all in. Bunnie and David, her parents, answered several questions about their own faith and their willingness to bring Sarah up in the nurture and love of God. A representative of the session, our governing body, stated the determination of the Church to provide for her care so that she in turn would come to know the love of God for her in Christ; and he said he hoped God would enable her in turn to profess her faith personally. The minister took her, baptized her by taking water in his hand and placing that hand on her head, and then prayed in our behalf for her growth in faith.[3] He then carried her down the center aisle of the sanctuary, speaking to her in a medium voice we could all hear: "Sarah, you will come to know in time what God provided for you in this hour, as you will come to know what God provides all your life. We remember as we baptize you that God's people care for us, that God's Spirit dwells in us, that God's grace infuses us with the presence of Jesus Christ. Sarah, in behalf of the Church universal, we pledge our faith, hope and love to you for your education in the faith, for your finding a world more in harmony with God's justice and purpose, and for your knowing God's presence throughout your life. Welcome and God bless you!"

Grandparents beamed from the front row. Children craned their necks to see the baby. Sunday School teachers made mental note of potential presence in years to come. And theologians such as I (oops, I mean historians) entered into a dialectic of praise and self-critical examination. "Is it too sentimental?" "How can God entrust so much to the Church?" "Woe is me." and so forth.

What I give to you is a personal testimony; that is the core of my message. Two years ago this congregation witnessed a more concrete example of the universal Church at work in baptism. Suraj and Rachel Alexander presented their daughter one Sunday—Priya Anne. Suraj had grown up in the Mar Thoma Church and Rachel in the Syrian Orthodox. Now parents were Presbyterian and grandparents visiting from India asked that a few extra customs be appended to the straight (stark?) Reformed worship.

Our minister, John Ames, preached that day on Exodus 3, the passage in which Moses receives a call from God to rescue the people of Israel from oppression. The other lesson came from John 17. John preached on the faithfulness of God and on participation in the Christian family. The sermon, "He Knows Our Name, Too," concentrated on the collaboration of Christians throughout the world to provide mission, evangelism, education, health care, and comfort so others may come to know God's love for them. "But don't forget," he implored, "that our responsibility begins with Priya Anne and those others whose nurture we pledge to provide." He closed with a word of thanksgiving.

I could keep going in this vein without apology. I honestly believe infant baptism can feed the people of God, that the ordinance or sacrament—call it what you will—is a celebration of vital Christian initiation. I believe it fits in the fabric of faith, a thread that helps make the fabric more durable, more beautiful, more harmonious.

I know beneath the instances and my own appreciation of them, however, lie some theological and historical questions that should be examined in this context as we study "Baptism, Eucharist, and Ministry." Let me just bow in the directions of several of these questions and issues:

1. Scriptural Authority
2. The Sequence of Faith, Repentance, and Baptism
3. The Process of Sanctification.

There are many more, but all three of these are important and addressing these issues will evoke discussion on
others. In examining each I want to keep the "argument"
personal and resist ethereal objectification.

Frankly, before I began research for this presentation, I
had considered the claims of believers' baptism Christians a
bit "cleaner" biblically than those of us who baptize infants.
In anticipation of my time with you I read again the arguments made by Karl Barth, as well as those of G. R. Beasley-
Murray; and I regained the pedobaptist modesty they formerly instilled.[4] However, this time I read also portions of
the J. Jeremias-K. Aland debate on liturgical practice in the
early Church.[5]

Previously I had taught seminarians, and followed in
my own consideration, what might be termed the "Sunday
analogy" as helpful for comprehending the matter of early
Church practice. Previously I had considered the evidence
from Scripture "mixed." Now instead of any "pure" evidence, I find the overall teaching "pure."

On the one hand, a real Jesus received baptism as an
adult (Matt. 3:15). On the other, he was baptized "in solidar-
ity with sinners to order to fulfill all righteousness." On the
one hand, Jesus called the little children to himself (Cull-
man argues *kōluein* was a liturgical term);[6] but Beasley-
Murray can equally argue the necessity of faith as a child's
faith is at stake in those pericopes. In the early Church,
Jewish proselytes' children were circumcised and baptized
upon the initiation of a family into the faith; alas, children
born after the conversion of their parents were not baptized.
Subsequent male children were merely circumcised. So it
goes—point, counterpoint.

Though such varieties among authorities might give
rise to cynicism, Geoffrey Wainwright offers a more constructive alternative:

The New Testament seems to favour now one, now another view of the relation between grace and faith in baptism, and sometimes the same passage is made to support opposing positions. Is it possible that the scholars are making upright but *mistaken* attempts to find a uniformity among texts which are genuinely divergent? Is the New Testament pattern one of a diversity in baptismal practice which reflects the rich variety of God's dealings with men and embodies more clearly now one, now another aspect of the fundamental mystery of the divine work of bringing people to salvation? Can it therefore be that the variety of positions adopted within and among the churches today is biblically justified? Will the One Church see several positions continue to be maintained, viewed as complementing each other rather than as mutually exclusive, with the circumstances in which the Church lives and prosecutes its mission determining the predominant practice in each situation?[7]

For my part, I commend the analogy of Sabbath observance as a way of comprehending authority patterns regarding infant baptism. Sunday worship obviously became a pattern for Christians that differed from religious habits in Judaism. Christian communions such as the Seventh-Day Baptists and the Seventh-Day Adventists have defined themselves over against the majority of Christians on the basis of Scriptural explicitness. One can today read concerted, well-researched polemics in favor of Sabbath worship versus "pagan acculturated habits" of the Sunday believers. But we "Sunday" Christians claim good, implicit authority from Scripture in behalf of our tradition. Historically, I have commended this analogy among fellow pedobaptists. Now I commend it also to Christian brothers and sisters depending upon the spiritual nourishment from believers' baptism.

Second, let us look briefly at the sequence in coming to discipleship. I am amused each time I lead a group of Presbyterian students through the sequence as the Westminster Confession of Faith describes it. Naturally, that sequencing takes form from the heavy reliance on the divines upon the eternal decrees of God, described in all their glory earlier in the document (Chapter III). Students will begin to fidget as I mention in turn "effectual calling," "justification," "adoption," and perhaps even "regeneration." Finally one will blurt out, "Wait a minute!" or "Hey, just a minute!" as we race through "saving faith" or "repentance into life." Even though they have read the Standards previously, the sheer logic of such a pattern becomes strained and almost impossible to comprehend. As we discuss the sequencing, we learn again that faith and repentance, assurance and adoption are so thoroughly interwoven for a Christian that any uniform sequencing gives difficulty indeed (if not incredulousness).

Therefore the sequence in which repentance and faith precede baptism does make sense. But other experiential sequencing makes sense as well, from Scripture and from experience as well as from Christian tradition.

The gifts of faith and repentance make more sense to me as I grow older (as I hope I grow more mature in both as well). Baptism does not seem necessarily tied to a particular point in the process, but rather it is a sacrament celebrating identification with Jesus Christ in the Church's perception of those gifts (as B.E.M. testifies).

Augustine, Nicolas of Cusa, John Calvin and many others resorted to a confession of *docta ignorantia* when they came to places of ambiguity in their work. Calvin used it in the *Institutes*, Book III, Chapter 21. He located predestination among the "ways we receive the grace of Christ."[8] Well, *docta ignorantia*, learned ignorance, seems an appropriate designation of my own movement in self-understanding regarding the rhythm and process of redemption. I invite all Christians to move toward such learned ignorance, a stance which does not celebrate knowledge or ignorance but rather celebrates a dawning of mature faith.

Thirdly, in just a word let me remind those of us believer baptists and pedobaptists of the general repudiation of the *clinici* (from *klinè*). We all perceive baptism as initiation in the faith, and we profess the process of sanctification as a subsequent process. Hence differences are quantitative, not qualitative, as we consider our theological stances.

I promised this would be primarily a personal testimony, and after my lengthy excursus into issues and theological positions, let me return to the personal level. When in junior high school, my best (male) friend was a Baptist. I accompanied him to youth group (was that a Training Union?). Anyhow, it was full of "sword drills" and such. I remember a big discussion at his home over dinner when another boy in the congregation was being considered for profession of faith and baptism. The minister, the board of deacons, and incidentally the family of my friend, all concurred in permitting him to be baptized along with the other young people his age. All my memories are hazy, but I now realize that the young man was, as we say, "considerably or profoundly retarded." Evidently he could not make more of an articulate profession of faith than that which someone could coach him to make at the proper occasion. Now I see the Christian action as theologically appropriate, beautiful in its comprehension of the grace of God in Jesus Christ, and scripturally defensible (as all Christian initiation upon profession of faith—whether familial, personal, or congregational). In providing for his baptism, that church did precisely what pedobaptists are accustomed to do.

In conclusion, I can witness to the consonance of infant baptism with the faith I profess and hold. I do not advocate infant baptism for all, but I do expect other Christians not to look down their noses at me and practices of the Reformed branch—B.E.M. is constructive and worth serious consideration.

"Baptism, Eucharist, and Ministry": How It Came to Be

LEWIS S. MUDGE

Dean
McCormick Theological Seminary

I am happy to be here today because no ecumenical achievement of recent years equals the importance, or the portent for the future, of the convergence text on "Baptism, Eucharist, and Ministry." That you, as representatives of "believers' churches" would decide to spend several days on this subject illustrates the impact of this ecumenical achievement.

There was a moment last week when Michael Kinnamon and I had the impression that we had been invited to speak on approximately the same topic. But we have conferred by phone and, I think, reached an understanding. I, for one, am particularly glad that Michael will be addressing you tomorrow morning. Michael had the invaluable experience of being on the World Council Faith and Order staff during the final stages of the B.E.M. process. He understands this topic exceedingly well. As for myself, I served at various times on the drafting group, and at Lima as that group's secretary. I was also present at Marseilles in 1972 when an early draft of what later became the Ministry document was hammered out, and at Accra in 1974.

Today I will try to do two things: first, to reflect on how B.E.M. as a whole came to be, and, second, to give some attention to the "Baptism" document in particular. This last is the place, as I understand it, where "believers' churches" find at least their initial difficulties. No doubt you find problems with the "Eucharist" and "Ministry" documents too, but I will barely touch on these this afternoon.

I.

How did B.E.M. come to be? I recommend the succinct account to be found in Appendix 1 of the volume of essays titled *Ecumenical Perspectives on Baptism, Eucharist and Ministry* edited by Max Thurian. The story of B.E.M. is told briefly there, with previously unpublished excerpts from some of the early drafts. In fact the whole Thurian volume is illuminating. Several of the essays, including my own on the "Baptism" document, give information about the drafting process in its ecumenical context. I call attention particularly to the piece by Gunter Wagner, himself a Baptist, titled "Baptism from Accra to Lima." This analyzes with great care the route by which the present "Baptism" document took form between 1974 and 1982. An approach to the subject with this kind of historical depth greatly helps us to understand the finished product.

B.E.M. as such goes back to a decision made in August, 1967, at the meeting of the Faith and Order Commission in Bristol, England. At that meeting the need was expressed for harvesting the areas of agreement reached by representatives of the churches at representing more than a generation of ecumenical dialogue. A meeting took place in October of that year which sought to make a more or less continuous text out of pronouncements on the Eucharist from Lund (1952), Montreal (1963), and Bristol (1967). A further draft of this "Eucharist" text went to the Faith and Order Working Committee at Uppsala (1968), and was further edited into a document titled "Beyond Intercommunion," which went to the Louvain Faith and Order Commission meeting of 1971, and then to Accra, 1974.

A text on baptism prepared in much the same way was proposed in 1970 and underwent further revisions prior to the Accra meeting. A draft on "Ministry" was prepared in June, 1972, for the Marseilles meeting which likewise drew up a text for Accra. It was at the Faith and Order Commission meeting in Ghana's capital that year that these three streams of effort came together. The text which became the "first edition" of B.E.M. began to take shape. The World Council Assembly at Nairobi in 1975 subsequently authorized the publication of *One Baptism, One Eucharist, and a Mutually Recognized Ministry* (Faith and Order Paper Number 73). This was the well known, beautifully illustrated booklet with the black and gold cover which had wide circulation in the churches in the late 1970s.

The member churches of the World Council and others were asked to study the Accra/Nairobi draft with care. There resulted a foot-high pile of responses from the churches, all of which was carefully analyzed and remitted to a series of drafting sessions under the chairpersonship of Frère Max Thurian of the Taize Community. This work eventually produced the material presented at Lima in January, 1982. I participated in two of these analyzing and drafting sessions, working especially on the Ministry document.

I do not expect you to remember all this detail. In fact there is much more, were the story to be fully told! But several general observations can be made. This was, in the first place, a very inclusive and including process. Membership in the Faith and Order Commission is not confined to representatives of member churches of the World Council which of course include the various Orthodox Commissions. Not only are the Roman Catholics now present in force, but representatives from "believers' churches," and particularly Baptists, are there as well. And comments on our drafts came from a still wider circle. Further, what began as simply an attempt to harvest results of work already accomplished turned into a project involving a great deal of fresh thinking and fresh drafting. The evolution of the "Eucharist" and "Ministry" documents, in particular, was spectacular. (The essentials of the "Baptism" document, by contrast, seem to have been there almost from the beginning. What evolved there was less a matter of content and more in the area of strategy. I will say more about this later.) The evolution of these documents was shaped by the growing participation of Roman Catholics in Faith and Order discussion, particularly after the Uppsala assembly of 1968. In that year we were almost euphoric about the prospect that Rome might actually join the WCC. The Louvain Commission meeting of 1971 saw Roman Catholic theologians taking a new and serious part in the process. Serious, indeed, because it was soon discovered that the Roman Catholics seemed to have a higher sense of responsibility for speaking and writing words which represent their church. No doubt they are more likely than many of us to be asked to explain, when they get home, why they said this or that at a given meeting! At any rate, Roman Catholic participation not only changed the center of gravity in dialogue. It also introduced a new style of doctrinal seriousness and competency into the discussion. This may account for what some have called the "catholicizing" tone of the result. Is this, perhaps, the price we pay for inclusiveness?

II.

If we compare the Accra/Nairobi draft (the famous black and gold pamphlet) with the Lima/Vancouver B.E.M. document, several other developments of general theological interest emerge. Accra/Nairobi is, in the first place, much more "sociological" than the formal B.E.M. text. One finds comments such as this:

> The Christian community always exists in a concrete sociological setting. Therefore, it cannot be described adequately in general theological terms. As we reflect on the nature of the community and on the place of the special ministry in the community, its actual sociological appearance must be taken into account.

Or consider the following:

> When the diversity of ordained ministry among the various churches is examined, it is evident that this diversity is bound up with the history and cultural particularity of those churches. Each case reveals what might be called a particular "theological-ecclesial culture."

Or, reflect upon this:

> Beyond their etymologies and dictionary definitions, words become the carriers of implicit metaphors, the vehicle of unconscious assumptions about human and relationships the functioning of social institutions derived from the cultures of different times and places. The taken-for-granted background of a given term often has its hidden influence on the way that term is combined with others to form more complex structures of thought. The same is true of the combination of symbolic acts to form liturgies.

Little of this "social scientific" overtone has survived into the present B.E.M. text. It proved offensive to the

Orthodox, and difficult for many Roman Catholics. The method of standing apart and looking at ourselves with social scientific or linguistic method proved utterly foreign to many of the discussants. We became aware that the Eastern churches, in particular, have never experienced anything comparable to the Enlightenment. The issue of how theology relates to sociology, and other human-science perspectives, remains unresolved in ecumenical discussion. I believe that the issue is of great importance.

A further evolutionary development took place in the wake of two seemingly innocent drafting decisions. The first was to restrict the length of the "Ministry" document to bring it more into line with the "Baptism" and "Eucharist" texts. The second was to distinguish throughout between main text and commentary, placing the principal assertions in one format and supplementing them with observations having, somehow, a lesser status. Both decisions led to results which many Protestants, including myself, sought to resist. It became evident to us that in shortening the "Ministry" text and in distinguishing between text and commentary, the drafters tended to exacerbate the "catholicizing" tendencies already noted. This particular Protestant, and no doubt others, felt that many of the things we wanted most to say had been either excluded from the "Ministry" document altogether, ostensibly to shorten it, or had been relegated to commentary. The result seemed to confirm the view that Protestantism is, at most, only a corrective *obligato* upon the main themes of Christian faith, without affirmations of its own deserving to be seen as integral to the Tradition as such. Several of us became very tired of metaphorically tugging at cassocks in order to be heard.

It is important for us all to know what the ecumenical situation really is and where we stand within it. Speaking as a Reformed theologian, I would say that we take the whole history of Christian Tradition as our own, but hold it as "reformed and always to be reformed." We do not see the doctrinal products of the Reformation as merely commentary on affirmations centrally defined by others. We would affirm that the doctrine of justification by grace alone, or of election to worldly vocation, combined with the tradition of prophetic witness for peace and justice in society, are strands which today are part of the fabric of the catholic faith. They need to be recognized as such by all who, with varying emphases, hold that faith.

Taken together, these points about the use of social scientific method on the one hand, and the status of Protestant affirmations within catholic tradition on the other, raise a fascinating issue. What is the *relation* between the perceptions and academic methods of modernity and Protestant witness as such? Has a certain sociological realism become the *instrument* of prophetic protest? To what extent do we wish to fight the battle as Protestants with the use of weapons derived from Max Weber or Jürgen Habermas, or even Karl Marx? If we do use these weapons, we lay ourselves open to the criticism that we have become "merely" sociological or secular. We feel the opprobrium of the Orthodox, who see our divisions and strongly suspect that they are the result of the entry of secularizing tendencies into our churches over a long period of time. But, on the other hand, the Protestant theologians tend to be much better acquainted with social scientific method than theologians of other traditions. By knowing the methods of modern secularity we can guard against the consequences of idolizing the world of which we are a part.

I would not wish Protestantism to be reduced to seeing the church as purveyor of liberal social analyses and general good works. The core of Trinitarian faith, lived in vivid evangelical awareness of Christ's presence within and among us, must remain. That said, however, I believe we have a vocation to use social analysis effectively and to bring such methods into dialogue with theology. Where will that lead us in future ecumenical discussions?

III.

The final lap in this already too-long discussion of B.E.M.'s genesis brings us to the Lima Faith and Order Commission meeting. On that occasion, in January, 1982, I served as secretary to the group charged with sorting out and recommending final action upon the numerous drafting suggestions made by members of the Commission and others. The B.E.M. text came to Lima, after years of work, in an advanced state of refinement. Still, there were 192 separate suggestions for change placed in the hands of our drafting group during the first week of the meeting! A rather large number of these were accepted in some form and subsequently enacted by the Commission. These facts, I think, indicate just how volatile the B.E.M. text was, especially in some sections, until shortly before the final vote on it was taken.

One would suppose that after so many years of effort this would not be so. Should we say simply that any piece of writing can always be improved and that when, to shift the metaphor, many cooks stir the broth, they are likely to want to slip in their favorite condiments? Yes, certainly, on both counts. But there is something more. The B.E.M. text is merely the evidence, the literary outcropping, of a process in which several hundred theologians of different Christian traditions, both members and consultants of the Faith and Order Commission and others who participated in the process, gained a degree of confidence in each other and in the validity of the ecumenical cause which made possible such a result in the first place. The verbal product of this process could well have been otherwise without being any the less valid. If we were to do it over again, the result *would* no doubt be different. But that is not the important thing. The important thing is that we have today reached a point of ecumenical development and momentum, as well as of spiritual communion with each other across Christendom, at which an enterprise of this sort can be accomplished. The words we write are important. I have elsewhere described them as "a fragile bridge of words between worlds." But they are not as important, perhaps, as their capacity to inspire meetings such as this one in which Christians ask what it means that such words exist at all.

IV.

You asked me to say a few words about the "Baptism" document. I am glad to do so as illustrative of the method of B.E.M. as a whole. The "Baptism" document contains basic biblical material presented in a form which distinguishes the meaning of the rite and its relation to faith on the one hand from actual practice in the churches on the other. It is this distinction which enables the document to transcend the historic tension between "believers' baptism" and other understandings of baptism. In the latter category there are basically two positions: that in which baptism is performed at any age, including infancy, and is followed immediately by admission to Holy Communion, and that in which baptism, usually in infancy, is merely the first stage in a process of initiation which leads to admission to Communion at the moment of taking on adult membership responsibilities. The basic meaning of baptism is laid out in five points with which few of us can disagree: (1) baptism is participation in Christ's death and resurrection, (2) conversion, pardoning, and cleansing, (3) the gift of the Spirit, (4) incorporation into the Body of Christ, and (5) the sign of the Kingdom. The

document then goes on to talk, in several crucial paragraphs, about baptism and faith. It is here that the heart of
the argument—permitting believers' baptism and other
forms of baptism to be seen in the same frame of reference—
occurs.

> The necessity of faith for the reception of the salvation
> embodied and set forth in baptism is acknowledged by
> all churches. Personal commitment is necessary for
> responsible membership in the Body of Christ.

Certainly this covers the whole range of possibilities,
although it also leaves much unsaid. In particular, one may
ask about the phrase "responsible membership." Is the reference to the Christian's ethical comportment or is it to
institutional involvement? Or both? Too little is said for the
reader to be sure.

The following paragraphs argue that, while we are at
one on the question of baptism's meaning and on baptism's
relation to faith, we carry out the implications of our beliefs
in several different ways. The strategy of the "Baptism"
document lies in this attempt to confine the difference
among us to questions of practice rather than faith, and to
exhibit our variety of practice as falling within a common
theological frame of reference. But is it not strange, in an age
such as this, to mute the claim heard on every side that faith
is expressed precisely *in* practice, in what we do and in the
way we do it? Different patterns of practice, especially when
they are seen in relation to social context, imply diverse
theological and ecclesiological understandings. It is hard to
believe that many of the drafters would deny this point.
Nevertheless, it is hardly recognized in the present text. Yet
the convergence of practices within our faith is eloquently
argued. An earlier generation of ecumenical drafting would

have said what could be said in common, and then would have reverted to the formula "some say this and some say that." Each major position would have been outlined in and for itself. Here, however, we find the positions woven into one exposition in such a way that they interpenetrate each other. They are made to seem like inevitable and complementary variances within one large scheme of understanding. Listen:

> Both the baptism of believers and the baptism of infants takes place in the Church as the community of faith. When one who can answer for himself or herself is baptized, a personal confession of faith will be an integral part of the baptismal service. When an infant is baptized, the personal response will be offered at a later moment in life. In both cases, the baptized person will have to grow in the understanding of faith. For those baptized upon their own confession of faith, there is always the constant requirement of a continuing growth of personal response in faith. In the case of infants, personal confession is expected later, and Christian nurture is directed to the eliciting of this confession. All baptism is rooted in and declares Christ's faithfulness unto death. It has its setting within the life and faith of the church and, through the witness of the whole church, points to the faithfulness of God, the ground of all life and faith. At every baptism the whole congregation reaffirms its faith in God and pledges itself to provide an environment of witness and service. Baptism should, therefore, always be celebrated and developed in the setting of the Christian community.

After such an affirmation it is not surprising that the commentary points to the possibility, already real in some communions, of combining both the infant-baptist and believer-baptist traditions, regarding the practices associated with them as equivalent alternatives for entry into the Church. This, in fact, is a possibility in the Presbyterian Church today. Are we on the brink of realizing that the historic distinctions between these two traditions, as soon as both are recognized to be valid, become distinctions without a genuine theological difference. Or are we still far from such a recognition?

The document goes on to make a point about which there has been much less sound and fury, yet still one of great importance. It is the point about a lapse of time between baptism and admission to Communion, or even between baptism and the rite marking the gift of the Holy Spirit. To administer the rite of baptism and yet to delay to a later date the admission of the person to Communion is an implicit denial of what baptism is, namely the rite of entry into membership in the Body of Christ. The underlying issue here is one little developed in the document but of major significance. What do we mean by "membership?" For some traditions "membership" is understood on the analogy of the family, or even of ethnicity. One enters upon such "membership" at birth, and baptism is then, in essence, a sign of what already is. For other traditions "membership" is understood on the analogy of the voluntary association or even of the possession of voting rights in a parliamentary body. In the latter case membership requires certain capacities and calls for the fulfillment of certain requirements which the community of membership plays down. The practice of baptism, then, depends not just on theological assumptions but on sociological presuppositions as well. The classical Troeltschian distinction between "church type" and "sect type" returns to haunt us. Questions of ecclesiology and not merely of the Sacraments become salient.

The document ends with a brief section on celebration of baptism which, I imagine, was felt by the drafters to be uncontroversial. But I can imagine the consternation of members of the society of Friends who find it stated, without qualification, that "baptism is administered with water in the name of the Father, the Son, and the Holy Spirit." The remark at the close of the commentary (actually a commentary on a paragraph other than this one) that "some African churches practice baptism of the Holy Spirit without water through the laying on of hands, while recognizing other churches' baptism," scarcely helps. The witness to baptism by the Spirit alone is not confined to "some African churches." While my own church has no such practice I have at least enough ecumenical imagination to understand the feelings of those who do.

These remarks have been somewhat critical. I believe that it is possible to have participated in the drafting of a text in good faith without being wholly satisfied with the result of the work. I believe it possible to be appreciative of the achievement B.E.M. represents while feeling free to say what one thinks of these writings in matters of details. To do the latter, indeed, adds credence to one's affirmation of the ecumenical process as a whole. One can stand for what one believes *within* the process, rather than standing outside of it.

V.

In closing, let me say a few words about how these texts are intended to be read. One cannot help but notice, first, that they are in classical, some would say stuffy, theological and ecclesiastical language. Where, we may ask, is the contemporary action-discourse? Where is the sensitivity to contextuality? Where is the evangelical witness? All the latter things, I would say are part of the driving force behind this product, even if they are muted in the product itself. But at the moment, the only language which will serve the purposes of a "convergence" text like this one is the classical Christian language.

Second, there is still a kind of open texture here. The term used in the preface is not "consensus" but "convergence." It is recognized that in these words we are coming closer to each other, but not that we have reached the point of being able to employ the same identical words. The term "consensus" is reserved for a stage of life together not yet reached: "that experience of life and articulation of faith necessary to realize and maintain the Church's visible unity." That deeper experience of life together is recognized as "a gift of the Spirit" which must be "realized as a communal experience before it can be articulated by common efforts into words." And, "full consensus can only be proclaimed after the churches reach the point of living and acting together in unity." I would note, by contrast, that the Consultation on Church Union *is* using the word "consensus" precisely because its goal is to achieve a form of life among certain particular churches which will exhibit the requisites of "visible unity" as outlined here.

Then how *is* this text to be taken if it is only evidence of a "convergence" and not itself a "consensus?" It is important to read carefully the question which the churches are being asked to answer as they move through the stages both of response to the B.E.M. document and of reception of it in faith and life. We are being asked to indicate the extent to which we "can recognize in this text the faith of the church through the ages . . . ." Or, to use words earlier in the Preface, to say how far this text can "become part of a faithful and sufficient reflection of the common Christian Tradition on essential elements of Christian communion." We are not being asked simply to say whether or not we like what we read here. We are not being asked to say only whether we agree with it, or whether we do things in our churches in the way B.E.M. suggests. We are being asked a much more important question. And that question is whether we "recognize" in this text something called "the faith of the Church through the ages." This last is something which belongs to no one church. Rather we are called to belong to *it*. We are asked to say whether we think B.E.M. begins to find words for that for which we do not yet have words: a tradition of faith by which we are all possessed even if we do not all use the same words when we express that tradition for ourselves and in terms of our own particular historical experience. This turns our usual question on its head. We are not asked to say whether the B.E.M. writers think as we do. We are asked, whatever we may be—Reformed, Roman Catholic, members of "believers'" churches—to see what happens when we try to think ecumenically as members of one body which, even now, is becoming visible. We are not all asked to think the same. We are rather asked to join in an articulation of that which holds us together in common. An exceptionally difficult task, to be sure. But one in which the hope for the ecumenical future resides.

"Baptism, Eucharist, and Ministry": Its Importance in the Search For Christian Unity

MICHAEL KINNAMON
Assistant Professor of Theology
Christian Theological Seminary

My task at this conference is to speak about the background of the World Council of Churches' document "Baptism, Eucharist, and Ministry" (B.E.M.), and to state clearly what the churches are now invited to do by way of response to this text. I must begin, however, by saying something about the wider ecumenical effort of which B.E.M. is a part.

During my time in Geneva I saw a number of people who acted as if the basic ecumenical question were, "How can we reconcile doctrinal disputes?" or "How can we co-operate more effectively in mission?" or even, "How can we merge church structures?" To my mind, the question which the ecumenical movement seeks to address is this: What does it mean to be the Church living in obedience to the will of God at this moment in the world's history? The ecumenically involved churches have insisted, for example, that the Church must be understood as a global fellowship. As Ernst Lange puts it in his excellent study, *And Yet It Moves*, the ecumenical movement *is* the movement of Christianity from the no longer tenable position of parochialism into the horizon of the *oikoumene*, the whole integrated earth.

Being more truly the Church, the ecumenical movement affirms, also means allowing God to work through us to confront and overcome such evils as racism and sexism and barriers of class in our fellowship. It is easy to overlook the fact that Paul spent as much time in his letters telling diverse kinds of people—especially Jews and Gentiles—how to live together in community as he did telling them how to preach the Gospel. Why? Because in Paul's vision the Church we are called to proclaim is precisely an "ecumenical" community. For me, this message culminates in Romans 15:7 where Paul exclaims, "Welcome one another as Christ has welcomed you for the glory of God." Why welcome one another—Jew and Greek, American and Russian, black and white? Because we have already been welcomed—accepted—by God despite our failings. And because through our life of diversity in community (so contrary to the way of the world) God is glorified.

The ecumenical vision of the Church, in other words, centers around a biblically-grounded spirituality that dares to live with differences in community. This demands, of course, a great level of trust which comes not as a result of polite tolerance but through our common commitment to and experience of Jesus Christ. In the United States there is a tendency today to think that those churches not involved in the ecumenical movement are characterized by the vigorous tenacity of their beliefs, while liberal, ecumenical churches are characterized by a kind of weak-kneed commitment to non-commitment. Or, as Martin Marty puts it, those who are committed aren't civil and those who are civil aren't committed. While there is unfortunately some truth in this caricature, I still think it is time to expose this falsehood by stating the ecumenical vision in a clear, integrated and dynamic way. Ecumenical Christians, at our best, are so committed to Jesus Christ that any separation from others who also are committed to him is really intolerable. Ecumenical Christians are so committed to God's mission that our inability to pray and act together on behalf of peace and justice in the world feels like the sin that it is. Ecumenical Christians are so committed to living the whole truth of the Christian faith that we readily admit that this truth is far greater than any of our separated witnesses. What distinguished ecumenical from nonecumenical churches is not that the latter are more committed to Christian truth but that the former maintain that a global, humanly-inclusive, socially-engaged community willing to live with differences *is* central to the truth of the Gospel.

The unity we are working and praying for, then, is a living communion of trust, sharing, and common service. We are to be a truly catholic community—diverse and universal—which celebrates with joy and thanksgiving God's saving acts, which calls people and nations to repentance, which announces forgiveness, and which denounces and opposes the war and injustice that deny God's plan for creation. Such communion does *not* depend on doctrinal agreement but on the experience of Christ in the Church, in the world, and in our hearts, and it may be that, for many people, this communion grows more through shared engagement in mission and service than through common confession.

Nonetheless, given our present state of ecclesial brokenness, the search for doctrinal consensus on certain fundamental issues can be a most important means for moving toward deeper, broader, truer communion. Being more truly the Church also means putting behind us, with God's help, those doctrinal disputes which go beyond diversity to division in order that we may give greater glory to our Creator, in order that we may be more visibly the reconciled community for which Christ prayed and, thus, a truer sign of God's active, reconciling presence in the world. B.E.M., and the many other efforts to achieve doctrinal consensus are not ends in themselves but tools for helping to lead us to living communion. B.E.M. does not aim at theological uniformity (we clearly must be able to live trustfully with a good deal of theological difference in Christian community); rather, it seeks to become a faithful and sufficient reflection of the common Gospel Tradition which will help us to see that we confess, despite great diversity, the same Jesus Christ. However you conceive the final goal of Christian unity, it would be vacuous without a basic common understanding on sacraments and ministry. As the former Director of the WCC's Faith and Order Commission, Lukas Vischer, has observed "Consensus on baptism is required so that everyone who receives baptism may know that he [or she] has been baptized with all the others into one and the same body of Christ. Consensus on the eucharist is required so that the whole people of God may be spiritually present at and participant in every celebration of the eucharist. Consensus on the ministry is required so that everyone who proclaims the Gospel may know that he [or she] stands in fellowship with all who have been called to the same ministry. Consensus [on these issues] is the precondition of real living fellowship."[1]

Having emphasized this broader context, and having stressed that B.E.M. is not an end in itself, but a tool for moving us into deeper fellowship, let me now rejoice for a moment. The past five years have witnessed greater theological convergence than most ecumenists dared dream possible just a generation ago; and B.E.M. is widely regarded as the most significant of these theological achievements for reasons I will offer in a moment. It certainly has generated more excitement than any previous Faith and Order study. The latest figures from Geneva indicate that the text has been translated, at local initiative, into eighteen languages, and that ten more translations are in process. Sixty thousand English copies have been sold from Geneva (and that doesn't take into account special English reprintings such as the one done by the Evangelical Association of Lutheran Churches). Fifty-five thousand German copies have been sold. And there is a growing body of secondary literature, much of it stemming from conferences such as this one. The spring 1984 issue of the *Journal of Ecumenical Studies* and the July 1984 issue of *Midstream* are both devoted entirely to B.E.M. This level of interest is a tribute to the importance of this document; it indicates that something new is happening in the search for Christian unity.

I.

I want to turn our focus now to the text itself by suggesting four reasons that B.E.M. deserves special attention and study throughout the Church.

1. This is definitely not a document rushed into print following some quickly-achieved compromise. B.E.M. is sometimes talked about as the product of a fifty-year study process in that the sacraments and ministry were already major topics of discussion at the first World Conference on Faith and Order in 1927. A special study on baptism was undertaken in 1952 and its report, "One Lord, One Baptism" (1960), became a cornerstone of the present text. Special studies on eucharist and ministry took shape during the 1960s. The three-part document was reworked by the Faith and Order Commission at its 1974 meeting in Accra, and was then sent for consideration to the WCC's Nairobi Assembly (1975) which decided, in turn, to send it to the churches for theological response. This was a most important step, one that not only greatly expanded participation in the study but also, in a sense, began the process of "reception." Replies were received from more than one hundred churches, in addition to some forty other bodies (e.g., councils of churches), and many of the suggestions were incorporated by a Steering Committee into later editions of the text. It is

unfortunate that, to my knowledge, only four Baptist groups—the American Baptist Churches in the USA, the Seventh-Day Baptist General Conference, the Baptist Union of Great Britain and Ireland, and the Baptist Union of Denmark—took the opportunity to respond to the Nairobi invitation.

Two Faith and Order consultations were also held in 1979 to deal with the particularly divisive issues of episcopacy and apostolic succession and believers' baptism. The conference on baptism, which is a kind of forerunner of this meeting, was held at the Southern Baptist Theological Seminary in Louisville. The final report, published in the Winter, 1980 issue of *Review and Expositor* (the theological journal of the Southern Baptist Theological Seminary), lists five major points of agreement:

- —believers' baptism is the most clearly attested practice of baptism in the New Testament, though infant baptism has developed with the Christian tradition and witnesses to valid Christian insights;
- —the personal faith of the recipient and continuous participation in the life of the Church are essential for the "full fruit" of baptism (in believers' baptism the believing community must play its part in the nurture of that faith from childhood, while in infant baptism, the believing community must nurture the child's faith toward personal confession and discipleship);
- —both forms of baptism require a similar and responsible attitude toward Christian nurture and a serious development of the Christian catechumenate;
- —the historical and social context of a church community influences its understanding and practice of baptism;
- —indiscriminate baptism is an abuse to be eliminated.

Those of you who have looked carefully at B.E.M. will probably be struck by how much of this language has found its way into the present version.

Finally, after these many years of preparation, the members of the Faith and Order Commission were asked at their 1982 meeting in Lima, Peru: Has this text reached sufficient "maturity" (is there sufficient convergence) that it should be transmitted to the churches for "official response" as part of a broader process of "reception." As you probably know, the answer was a unanimous "yes."

Before moving to my next point, I want to be careful to say exactly what happened in Lima. The Commission did not "approve" the B.E.M. text—that is something only the churches can do. And not every member would agree with every line. But it was clear that the commissioners, with two or three exceptions, felt this to be a balanced, mature statement which basically reflects the apostolic faith of the Church and is sufficient to move us to the next stage in the search for unity. And some of them, of course, would claim a far greater achievement. Jürgen Moltmann has stated bluntly that, "After fifty years of concerted theological effort we now have to say quite openly to Christians and church authorities that there are no longer any doctrinal differences which justify the divisions of our churches. . .Of course much work still remains to be done on each of these central points of the faith, but what remains can only be done together."[2]

2. My second point is sure to get me in trouble here, but I think it is true nonetheless. B.E.M. also deserves special attention because of the group that produced it. The Faith and Order Commission of the WCC is, quite simply, the most confessionally and culturally comprehensive theological forum in the Christian world. The 120 members at the time the commission met in Lima included Roman Catholic

scholars (despite the fact that the Roman Catholic Church is not a member of the WCC as a whole) as well as Lutherans, Anglicans, Methodists, Presbyterians, Eastern and Oriental Orthodox, representatives from United Churches, Baptists, Disciples, Waldensians, Pentecostals, and Seventh-Day Adventists. . . . And they represented all parts of the world. Baptists in the Lima commission came from Nigeria, Burma, Jamaica, Switzerland, and England, as well as both the American and Southern Baptist Conventions in the United States. The B.E.M. preface is not wrong when it argues that it is unprecedented in the modern ecumenical movement for theologians of such widely varied traditions to speak so harmoniously on fundamental matters of doctrine.

Having said this, I acknowledge that Brethren, Church of God, Mennonites, and Quakers (among others) were not represented on the commission in the years between Nairobi and Lima. I regret these omissions, but they do not invalidate my earlier claim that Faith and Order is the most comprehensive forum yet established; they simply underline the importance of the current reception process in which meetings such as this one may be able to expand the community of those involved in this effort. Beyond that, I would remind us that some parts of the Radical Reformation unfortunately refuse to participate in ecumenical theological conversations, at any level, despite repeated overtures. I personally invited leaders of the relatively large Plymouth Brethren community on the Faroe Islands to respond to B.E.M. The answer was a polite but firm refusal.

3. B.E.M. is also of special significance because of the methodology used to produce it. Until the 1950s, Faith and Order was a place where the churches compared their conceptions of doctrinal issues (which obviously put Disciples, Baptists, and others at a disadvantage). But the real problem with this old "comparative ecclesiology" method is that it

reinforces a self-satisfaction with the riches of our own traditions instead of a longing for the fullness which each tradition inevitably lacks. The real breakthrough seemed to come in 1963 at the Fourth World Conference on Faith and Order in Montreal where a crucial distinction was made between "traditions" and "Tradition," and where the delegates spoke about the goal of ecumenical theology as a recovery of the "Tradition of the Gospel, testified in Scripture, transmitted in and by the Church through the power of the Holy Spirit." Not *sola scriptura* but the living witness of Scripture as it has found embodiment in the Church through the power of God's Spirit. Our job, Faith and Order said in effect, is not to compare twigs and branches of the Christian tree, but to explore *together* the common trunk—a methodology which should basically appeal to believers' churches. The goal of this work, in other words, is not simply to get Orthodox and Baptists and Presbyterians and Lutherans together, and certainly not to reach a polite compromise, but to understand what it means to be the Church, celebrating and experiencing God's gift in Christ through a sacramental life and participating in God's plan for creation through ministry in Christ's name. B.E.M. takes the truth of Christian proclamation most seriously, but suggests that several disputes over this truth which once divided our fellowship need no longer do so.

I have lifted up this methodology because it points us toward what I think is the crucial question for all churches as they study and respond to this text: Are the churches willing to allow their understandings of the faith to be measured by this most significant ecumenical attempt to articulate the Tradition of the Gospel, or will they insist on judging this result of ecumenical study by their confessional standards? This is a very fine line to walk. Of course the churches must "evaluate" B.E.M. in light of what they take to be fundamental articles of faith; but they must also be willing to allow B.E.M. to evaluate them. They must be open to the possibility that the Spirit is leading us to recover and express the faith of the apostles in new ways, ways that may differ from or add to or revise previous confessional formulations. I have heard Lukas Visher lament that when ecumenical work happens to agree with our tradition we term it highly significant; when it does not, we call it insufficiently developed. B.E.M. calls that bluff as no previous ecumenical document has ever done. For the first time we confront each other world-wide in the presence of a theological text that offers a common understanding on old issues of division.

Another way to put this point is to say that when I spoke on B.E.M. in Scandinavia, the one question I would not entertain was "How Lutheran is it?" (Or as another former Faith and Order Director, William Lazareth, puts its, the issue is not how Lutheran is Lima but how orthodox is Augustana.) In Rome, I felt defeated if people insisted on asking if it conformed to the Council of Trent. I would hope that our churches have slightly less need of this caution. The goal must be to struggle together to confess the Tradition of the Gospel, not simply to preserve intact our confessional traditions. If that happens as a result of B.E.M., then we are already at a new stage on the ecumenical journey.

4. Finally, I think that B.E.M. is of special significance because it presents, and at times even stresses, the crucial relationship between sacrament and service, between worship and mission, between doctrine and a life of obedience. The baptism section speaks of Christ as "the Liberator of all human beings" and observes that our baptism, "as a baptism into Christ's death, has ethical implications which not only call for personal sanctification, but also motivate Christians to strive for the realization of the will of God in all realms of life" (B 10). The Ministry section proclaims

that "Jesus made his own nature, condition and cause of the whole human race, giving himself as a sacrifice for all." He offered (and continues to offer) salvation to sinners, good news to the poor, release to captives, sight to the blind, and liberation to the oppressed; and the text makes clear that our ministry in his name should do the same (M 1 and 4).

It is in the section on eucharist, however, that this theme finds its most forceful expression. The Christ, whose real and living presence we encounter at the Lord's Table, is understood as the servant who went out to publicans and sinners during his earthly ministry, and who gave himself on the Cross for the sake of the whole world. B.E.M. places great emphasis on the activity of the Holy Spirit, but it stresses that the prayer of *epiclesis* or invocation is not only concerned with the bread and wine but it is a prayer that the faithful gathered around the Table may be transformed by the Spirit and, thus, empowered to fulfill their mission in the world (E 17). The eucharist, understood in this way, demands a change in the quality of relationships within the Christian community. "All kinds of injustice, racism, separation and lack of freedom are radically challenged when we share in the body and blood of Christ" (E 20). And the text does not stop with internal Christian relations. "The eucharist," it says, "involved the believer in the central event of the world's history. As participants in the eucharist, therefore, we prove inconsistent if we are not actively participating in this ongoing restoration of the world's situation and the human condition" (E 20). Until the full advent of the Kingdom, members of Christ's body, nourished and inspired by the bread and wine of his Table, must be actively committed to changing this world in the direction God wills. Given the privatized, spiritualized approach to the sacraments taken by so many churches in the past, I find this a refreshing and challenging development.

II.

Since returning to the United States, I have discovered a good deal of uncertainty about what the churches are now invited to do with this document. It is important to realize that the WCC has requested two related but distinguishable things: *official response* as part of a larger process of *reception.*

With regard to official response, the Council has invited all churches that wish to participate (and especially those that are members of the WCC and/or are represented on Faith and Order) to prepare answers, at the highest appropriate level of authority, to four questions, including the following:

—To what extent can your church recognize in this text the faith of the Church through the ages?
—What consequences can your church draw from this text for its relations and dialogues with other churches, particularly with those churches which also recognize the text as an expression of the apostolic faith?

The Vancouver Assembly of the WCC stressed that these answers, which are to be sent by the end of 1985, should not be "simply the response of individuals or groups within the church, but are, in some sense, understood by the church itself, given on behalf of the church."

Please note what a fine line the WCC is walking when it speaks of this official response. On the one hand, it wants to say that something much more than another round of theological discussion is now called for and expected. We can talk about the "goal" of unity forever without demanding much of the churches. B.E.M. suggests that the time has come for ecumenism to make a real difference in our ecclesiastical and ecclesiological life. The theologians have said, in effect, that there is no good reason why we cannot put most of the historic disputes over the sacraments and ministry behind us. The official response is a chance to test this perception.

But, on the other hand, the Council does not want to imply that December 31, 1985, is a time for a final yes or no decision on B.E.M. The question is not whether B.E.M. is a perfect document but whether the convergence it represents is sufficient (undoubtedly with some modification) to move us into deeper fellowship, to move us to a mutual recognition of members and ministries and more regular sharing of the Lord's Supper. This particular document, in other words, is no longer open for revision as it was before Lima (that could have gone on forever), but the process is open.

In terms of actual timeline, the Faith and Order Commission will review the responses during 1986 in order to prepare the agenda for another World Conference on Faith and Order, now proposed for 1987 or 1988. That conference, the first for Faith and Order since 1963, would be the time for announcing whether or not the theological convergence has actually led us toward ecclesiastical agreement. It would also be a time, I hope, for hearing new voices in this discussion. Churches not represented in the WCC or Faith and Order are, indeed, most welcome to prepare responses which will feed into preparations for the World Conference. This might be an excellent time to introduce parts of your fellowships to the serious theological work currently underway in the ecumenical movement, and to contribute directly to that work.

All that I have said so far indicates why the official response must be seen in a wider framework. I understand the term "reception" to mean an ongoing process of communication and education within a church through which its members are helped to evaluate and, as far as possible, embrace a given formulation (in this case B.E.M.) as an expression of the apostolic faith. I have seen several studies related to B.E.M. which explore the term "reception" in the history of the Church, describing, for example, how the Nicene and Chalcedonian confessions were received by the churches. But, in my opinion, such studies are a bit off target. The WCC is not a council like Nicea or Chalcedon. What we are involved in now is a reception process undertaken by still-divided churches, one which must rely on ecumenical trust, on the will to unity, on broad-based study by congregations, seminaries, and ecumenical commissions. The point is not to seek canonical endorsement, but to initiate a process of study and decision which will inspire ecumenical action.

I hardly need to observe that the process associated with B.E.M. is presenting different kinds of problems for different churches. Congregational churches, as many of you will know, have difficulties with the idea of official response. Who has the authority to speak theologically to and for our fellowships? The Disciples have worked out a procedure that will lead to an official response from our General Board, but it is clear to everyone that when Indianapolis speaks it does not have the same weight as when Rome speaks. Faith and Order must find some meaningful way to compare responses.

On the other side of the coin, the hierarchially-structured churches always run the risk of having their magisterial authorities issue a response which prevents or undermines real encounter with a text at the local level. This happened in Rome with regard to the report of the Anglican-Roman Catholic theological commission, but it has not happened with regard to B.E.M. Still, there is no doubt that the study of ecumenical materials co-authored by persons outside their churches presents a new challenge for the exercise of magisterial instrumentalities.

The bigger problems, however, are far more intangible. Some churches have allowed secondary issues of discipline and aesthetics to become the barriers surrounding their ecclesiastical houses. Many of us have a fear of losing a comfortable sense of identity and entrenched privilege. We have all grown used to demanding levels of agreement from ecumenical partners that we do not dare demand in our own fellowships. The ecumenical vision requires nothing less than repentance and a willingness to experience transformation on the part of all our churches, as we seek to be the Church living in obedience to the will of God.

Teaching and Preaching Issues For Believers' Churches Arising from the B.E.M. Document

LAUREE HERSCH MEYER

Associate Professor of Biblical Theology
Bethany Theological Seminary

We have shared our history, theology, and practice of baptism with one another in these last days. As I listened to the presentations I noted that our theologies and practices *form* our people; they also guide our *con-formation* or common discipline; and they move our hearts and imaginations, so that we are *re-formed* into ministers able to link together God and God's people in critical life situations.

Churchly discussions surrounding baptism, eucharist, and ministry tend in one of two directions. Christians sometimes measure the B.E.M. document by their ecclesial confession and practice, asking whether the document is adequate or faithful to their understandings. Such reflection encourages equating each ecclesial heritage and understanding with *the* Christian theology and practice. Where Christ is Lord, dissent about practice has marked the Christian heritage at least since Peter and Paul's rather heated disagreement. Unity in Christ does not depend on, nor is it necessarily achieved by harmony in matters of ecclesiology, theology, or polity.

A second way of addressing the B.E.M. document is for churches to receive it as both a call and a witness to our common faith. This approach invites us to measure our confessions and practices by the commitment the document represents. We are then encouraged to ask wherein our treasured inheritances have come to be mis-taken as God's truth. Our inheritance is very easily viewed as our "possession." In the B.E.M. document God calls us, like Abraham, to choose whether we more fully trust our particular ecclesial signs of promise, or God, our promisegiver.

My reflections follow this second approach. I think of this as attending to the backside of our denominational, theological glory. The document is of course no measure of our faithfulness. It does call us to take seriously our membership in Christ's church and converse with one another as those who are also members of the body of Christ, also called to bear common witness to our Lord in the disparate life situations in which each is placed.

My reflections involve three steps. First, I shall recall a story you know quite well. Second, I name recurring issues related to our theologies and practices of baptism. Third, I relate these familiar issues to those "alien" practices and theologies of baptism important to Christians not of our traditions. In that third move, I note some contexts and limits of confessional identities. I do not ask how some universally normative knowledge of baptismal validity other than confession of faith in Jesus Christ is possible. Rather, I inquire how the baptismal theology and practice of multiple communions illumines our particular ecclesial inheritance and identity. I believe this posture allows us to receive the B.E.M. document and converse openly regarding our common call to make manifest our unity in Jesus Christ.

I.

You remember the wonderful Exodus story. Perhaps you also shuddered on first hearing the golden calf story in

Exodus 32–34. Well, tucked away between the golden calf story and Israel's second set of Torah tablets is an important, rarely attended story. I retell these stories to help us see the backside, the unattended stories within this story. The unattended stories of Scripture are ours as well as the commonly known stories. Unattended stories may help us note the unintended results, the backsides, of our theologies and practices of baptism.

You recall the setting: Israel is out of Egypt, located in the wilderness about Sinai. The people have thrice declared they will "do the words of the Lord," (Ex. 19:8b; 24:3c; and 24:7c). Israel wants to be Yahweh's people and know Yahweh as its Lord. Moses has gone up to Yahweh. It was a long visit, forty days and nights. The number alone alerts us to immanent trouble. Sure enough, Israel acted to fill the vacuum created by Moses' absence.

Acting on their own is not exactly what we have in mind when we talk of all members as being the priesthood of all believers. But there it is. Their set-apart leader too long unavailable, Israel called Aaron to lead a self-styled celebration. They wanted to worship and rejoice over their deliverance from slavery. But, although their bodies were delivered from slavery, their memories and imaginations were still enslaved. They could only imagine celebration according to their age-old slavery experiences. Deliverance memories arising from their freshly-made covenant with Yahweh had not yet informed their imagination.

When Israel celebrated deliverance without Moses' guidance, it worshipped falsely because it was formed falsely. We, as Israel, worship with the images of whatever formed us. Israel's action made visible its dilemma: committed people must express their convictions in images which arise out of what they know well.

In Moses' absence, Israel interpreted its exodus experience and new covenant in light of its early formation. It had just covenanted to do all *Yahweh's* words, but Israel's con-fession had not become internalized. We know the dilemma at baptism, marriage, and in ecumenical conversations; we make commitments into which we have yet to grow. Israel had made a commitment to be God's people, but its internal identity was still that of newly-freed slaves. Left to ourselves, we express ourselves in images we most deeply know, whether that be images of God or of unreliable gods. Even images of deep-rooted and hated memories, when anchored in earlier landscapes of our life, hold power over us.

In Exodus, Israel received glorious deliverance. The backside of deliverance was that, though free *from* slavery, Israel was not free *as* God's people. Thus, Israel was not yet free to serve, to minister, to worship in God's name. We know so well the backside of Israel's exodus story that we sometimes feel more contempt than compassion toward Israel when telling it. When we get stuck on Israel's disobe-dience, we overlook the awe-filled interchange between Moses and God which follows it.

God noticed Israel's idolatrous response, and flew into a rage. God proposed to Moses that Israel be destroyed. God would then make of Moses a great nation. But Moses stepped between God and Israel, averting God's fury.

Amazing.

Is this the Moses whom God cajoled into shepherding Israel rather than Jethro's flock? How well Moses learned! Now Moses will not let even *God* prey on this foolish flock. Moses held God to the old covenant with Abraham when Israel showed no evidence of being children of promise. We could be ironic and note that since Moses was also a child of Abraham, Moses would surely die if God relinquished that ancient promise. And if Moses lived, would he not wonder whether God might not, generations later, reject Moses for a new hero if Moses' descendants' were to sin? Irony serves us poorly. If Moses is to trust God, both God *and* Moses must cleave to Israel in its faithlessness.

Moses risked trusting that God would be God, that God would save and not destroy faithless Israel. Had God rejected Israel now, Moses would have been without people or God. In the crucible of Israel's crisis, Moses experiences crisis. And Moses measures up. The hero became a minister. An obedient servant of Yahweh who delivered Israel from slavery, Moses now becomes a compassionate servant connected with God and Israel in their hostility. Moses saw that Israel's covenant with God did not "make" Israel God's servant; covenant initiated Israel's pilgrimage to become God's people. Israel's hearts were not yet steeped with memories and images of Yahweh; so in times of fear, chaos, stress, they turned to what they knew. They did not yet know the very Yahweh to whom they had covenanted their lives.

How are images of the heart changed? Perhaps Moses remembered that, measured by obedience and perfection, *his* formation was as rotten as Israel's. But, even as Israel in his absence, he had been passionate; he had been able to act! He had paid a high price; so would Israel. But he had become God's servant; so could Israel. He had had help from Jethro and others; and he could be that help for Israel.

Moses held God to God's promise that Israel was already chosen as God's people. Moses, who earlier and reluctantly became God's obedient servant as Israel's heroic deliverer now became Israel's compassionate servant as God's tenacious interpreter. During external crisis, Moses went to Israel as a God-sent advocate; in response to internal crisis, Moses became Israel's minister: a leader who links God and God's people together amid life's multiple crises. Moses abandons neither God nor Israel. Called to deliver God's people amid external crisis, Moses delivers people and God to one another when Israel and Yahweh seemed wilder enemies than was Egypt.

Moses' glory has its backside too. Moses goes down the mountain to make it clear that Israel was not abandoned although its impulsive actions would have painful consequences. Israel is sincere. And naive. Nonetheless, how Israel worships and behaves *matters.* Commitment to Yahweh cannot be nurtured from non-Yahwistic memory and imagination. Commitment requires self-discipline, self-enrollment toward growth. Whose people Israel is, is known by whether, under stress, Israel remembers in its heart Yahweh or their old images.

After dealing with Israel, Moses returns to Yahweh for a second set of tablets. God has cooled down now. Too much, in fact. God will let Israel live, but has lost personal interest. An angel will be sent along to provide protection on Israel and Moses' journey to the land of promise. Moses will not hear of that. An absent God is as worthless as a people with false imagination. If God will not go with them on pilgrimage, Moses will not depart. A godless people is no people, angels not withstanding. Finally, God agrees to go along. After all, he knows Moses by name. Deep friendships move Yahweh as well as us mortals.

It has been a rough day for Moses. He seeks a sign that reconciliation with Yahweh is accomplished; he asks to see God's glory. This Moses, who used to talk with God face to face, who argued God out of killing Israel and pressed Yahweh to journey along to the land of promise, this Moses asks to see once more God's glory. But now Moses is not permitted to see God's face. He may now see only the backside of God's glory (Ex. 33:23).

When ministers become the link between God and God's people, the old glory of uncomplicated certainty is gone; we dwell in the backside of glory. Great heroes of faith may see God's face; but great servants of faith live with the backside of glory. Ministry is rooted in compassion, a deep connection with both God and God's people, a compassion averted neither by faithlessness nor fury.

The frontside of glory features great promise, certain hope, theological vision. The frontside of glory dares speak normatively of truth, doctrine, ethics, theology; it gives logical proofs of these claims.

The backside of glory directs us to the ambiguity of experience: our mixed formations, our compromised realities, our betrayed or misunderstood commitments. The backside of glory confesses how deeply contextual are all expressions of faith and practice. There is a universal validity of belonging to God in Jesus Christ; there is no universal proof of valid faith and practice. The backside of glory does not prove; it describes events, tells stories, and links people and God with compassion.

II.

We look now to the backside of our own stories. We have told one another of our history, theology, and practice regarding baptism. We addressed a number of issues repeatedly. Those I heard most often were:

1. As we addressed our baptismal theology and practice, we gave particular attention to "issues" for pastoral care. We experience these "issues" as the backside of our theology, indications that we do not fully embody our theology—or that our theology is in transition. Our theological confessions were usually presented as normative, while practice statements were usually presented descriptively. When theology and practice were found in tension with one another, we usually assumed that our practice needed to be corrected by our theology.

2. There was reference in a number of presentations to "stages" of growth and faith, and to rites of passage. I prefer and will use the word "terrains" of perception and experi-

ence to refer to these "stages." We seem to never grow out of a "stage" or terrain of faith, though new perceptions and experiences may be added to us. In the last section, I will refer to these terrains as formation (which precedes our conscious intent), con-formation (cooperating with or intentionally opposing formation), and re-formation (giving into new form and experiencing our values).

3. Context and socio-cultural influence was acknowledged as significant. We spoke of second generation experience in community, and the move from socially over-against to a more self-invested posture among free churches. We were not agreed on how we thought all this mattered; we were clear that it did. For instance, church-world separatism is common to our ecclesial experience and is variously expressed in our baptismal theology and practice. Yet while many believe faithfulness requires that we always be over against the world, we do not equate that with a blanket rejection of culture. We know faith in Jesus Christ is incarnated in each time and place. This recognition leads us to recognize that both change and continuity mark faithful theology and practice, both in baptism and in all other marks of Christian life and practice.

4. We struggled with many questions of validity and truth. Was the meaning of baptism the same for Jesus as for the early church? Though baptism may signify entrance into public ministry for Jesus and for us, we saw that into and for what *he* was baptized was not the same as what Matthew 28:19–20 calls for, nor the same as for us today. If continuity between Jesus' baptism (or that of the early church) and ours is central, of what does that continuity consists?

We also saw that we appeal to Scripture to validate *some*, but not all, of our practices and theology. How is it that we change the measures by which we validate our theology and practice: now Scripture, now being over against the world, now finding how best to express a thing in changed life contexts? We validate our faith by different measures, depending on whether we address the theology and practice of baptism, the office and practice of ministry, the holding of common or personal property, relations to governmental authority, etc.

When we remember the story of Exodus 32-34, we recall that different persons in the same event experience and interpret it differently. Likewise we "same" people at different times in our lives in faith experience and interpret events differently. Thus some of us heard the B.E.M. document read as a normative statement, while others heard in it a contextual, confessional statement. I believe much Christian argument about baptism arises because we make universal, normative claims for that which has its origin in faith as a contextual or incarnate confession.

I do not suggest that the conceptual, theological, visionary, and ordering tasks of the church are secondary. But, in its oldest christological declarations, the church has insisted that theology and practice, divine and human, transcendent and immanent belong together in Christian faith. The backside of great theological vision is its practical limits; the backside of folk theology is its reflective limits. Conceptual theology rarely attends to the context which limits its thought. Thus, when theological reflection universalizes its content, other contexts and confessions are subordinated in order to "establish" its truth. We are just learning that for God to be incarnate in those cultures, Jesus *is* Black, Asian, Hispanic. Biblical story always contextualizes the universal; it does not universalize its contextual confessions.

III.

In relation to imagery from biblical and personal story, let me draw analogical terrains in which to look at major Christian contexts, confessions, and issues surrounding baptism.

In Christian life and faith, baptism has been practiced in multiple terrains. All Christian communions have heritages filled with glory and ambiguity, frontsides and backsides. Free church folk are often inclined to remember the pain and injustice of our heritage or of our current experiences as if socio-ecclesial limits, rather than God's promise, were our inheritance. Orthodox, Catholics, and Reformation Christians are more inclined to remember their formative and confessional practice and affirmations as if they were the normative content and context of all Christian faith and practice. None of us can serve two inheritances. Whether remembering injustice done to us or remembering truth given us, we are called to look beyond our contextually incarnate heritage or limits, for Jesus Christ, our common life and hope, calls us in our many cultures and experiences to unity in and as God's incarnate Body.

Christians choose Jesus Christ. But Christians also get caught in the backside of contextual ambiguity. We are often tempted to "do" theology from the glory or agony of our experience. Life is full of ambiguity, and commitment and service occur in its midst. When we first confront the old, old question, "How can we believe in a good God when life is full of injustice, pain, and chaos?," we realize that by the measure of suffering, Jesus' life, and the disciples' and church's faith, are foolish.

In Jesus Christ, God is with us; God dwells with and renews all creation; God is incarnate in forms and faith we find alien, as in experiences we know as hostile. Baptism in multiple forms, given in multiple ways and at multiple ages,

is one bond which holds together God and God's people in
Jesus Christ and the life of the Holy Spirit.

In baptism, we fundamentally confess Jesus Christ, not
this or that baptism into Jesus Christ. Our inheritance in
Jesus Christ is our confession of life, of hope, of unity. Like
Peter (Jn. 21:21), we are inclined to receive Jesus' invitation
to us, and then turn to Jesus and say, "But what of him? of
her? of another confession's faith and practice?" And Jesus is
likely to say to us believers' church baptizers as he is to infant
baptizers, "What is that to you? Come, follow me." Members
of the same body have the same inheritance: to be heirs and
children of God. But as some are toes, and others arms, and
other kneecaps, we are more called to serve the body than we
are to determine whether toes and arms are proper toes and
arms unless they are the same baptism as kneecaps.

In the great diversity among Christians regarding baptism, what is our *common* meaning? Our practice actually
addresses three major terrains of "belonging" in Jesus
Christ. One is *formation*, that experience of enrolling into
the community children born to its members, and surrounding them with the nurture in story, imagery, experience
which embodies God's story for their lives.

Second is *con-formation*, that experience of receiving
covenant and pledging commitment in order to become
heirs and disciples in the faith and practice of a particular
people of God. Here is the terrain of belonging, of receiving
identity and worth, of discovering one's gifts and limits, of
testing what it means to "do God's words" in this community, time, and place. It is also a time of being tested by the
events and experiences of personal and common life, of
learning how the values and practices of this community
enable us to live as God-bearers in times of crisis.

The third is *re-formation*, that experience of regiving to
the lives of those about us the identity, commitment, com-

passion which we have received. Precisely in those situations where pain, ambiguity, and crisis let us feel how death threatens life, that chaos may invalidate promise, service and ministry are crucial. At times like the golden calf story, or when we argue who is right or wrong in Christian faith and practice, leaders are needed who can re-direct people's faith *to* God *in* crisis rather than letting crisis set the terms for faith. Nurture and obedience are a necessary basis for service, but the ability to re-direct or re-form faith's expression for each new age and place is also crucial.

These three terrains are three faces of the same experience. People of all ages may experience and do need what is characteristic of all terrains. These are not stages we go through; they are terrains we indwell, perceive, and offer one another.

Thus, children, as all of us at times, need *nurture* in order to grow into the fullness and joy able to commit ourselves. It is like falling in love; we can marry without love, but the stress of marriage stands a better chance of giving life if the committed partners feel full of life and love. Inasmuch as and wherever we are needy, we "are" in the experiential terrain of formation. Formation nurtures by assuring us that we are members of God's people, heirs whose neediness does not invalidate our participation in God's life: which *is* our life.

Likewise adolescents, as all of us at other times, need discipline to guide our intentional self-commitment that we may test, grow in fullness the covenants we make, and renew commitment again and again with Jesus Christ. Conformation is also like love: like love which has given itself in covenant, and always needs both nurture and discipline as we learn what it means to belong to one another. Conformation is testing and being tested as we discern the limits of independence and uniformity in shared identity.

Moreover adults, like all of us at times, need to give ourselves to and be received as servants whose ministry fulfills others. Our common life in Jesus Christ is our call to serve all creation as stewards, ministers, servants of God who bring God's love into human brokenness, fear, and hostility.

Formation, conformation, and re-formation occur in every event of human life. Israel needed nurture; both it and Aaron needed discipline in the golden calf episode. Though Moses was a servant who gave himself in that episode, he also sought renewal and nurture. We can recall moments when Moses failed as servant (cf. The waters of Meribah, Num. 20) even as we sometimes fail ourselves and our communities. "Adult" servants who are able to identify God's new hope in chaos are also "children" needing nurture and "adolescents" needing self-discipline and testing.

In Scripture, in the ancient church, and in the church today, each of these three terrains has been recognized as having liturgical importance to personal and corporate life. We can call these infant, adolescent, and adult rites of passage. We can illustrate them with circumcision, Bar Mitzvah, marriage, and property-holding. Among believers' churches, we practice child dedication, youth training/baptism, and baptism as ordination into the priesthood of all believers.

Baptism has been practiced by Christians in each terrain. Each has significance and limits as well as tasks appropriate for leaders and members. The enrollment of infants into God's people is akin to the Abrahamic covenant. The leadership task for those received by baptism into Christian formation is to see that God's promised inheritance and gift of grace assured by adoption into God's family is offered, again and again, to all adopted by baptism into the family. Liturgy in family and churchly life, and stories and conversations of faith, as well as compassionate responses to persons in the face of whatever overwhelms, embody God's unconditional grace to those in formation.

The "task" of those in formation is to give voice to their experience: to be honest about what they feel, to be open to respond to what life brings them. Leaders can be overconcerned with the needs characterizing one terrain, and overlook the needs of another. The body will then suffer. The concern central to formation is that children feel loved just as they are, and feel themselves secure in a warm, trustworthy community.

The enrollment of intentional obedience which tests and is tested amid life's dangers and ambiguity is akin to the wilderness trials which follow the Sinai covenant. In conformation, members need to discern what imagery and behavior directs this community. They test and are tested, con-forming to or disassociating their identity from current corporate identity and limits. To risk such testing, members need to feel they belong and have gifts cherished by the body. Self-discipline and limit-setting are possible when one feels one's gifts are discerned, called forth, received as important to the community. Personal and corporate identity become one as shared disciplines, celebration, and experiences of being mutually important to one another are at the center of corporate pilgrimage.

The task of leadership in con-formation is to give compassion and direction, to set limits while naming and receiving others' gifts. Thus "leaders" and "members" test and are tested in relation to the common commitment to and discipline all have in Jesus Christ. In this terrain leaders are needed who guide without dominating or abandoning. Con-formation concurs in wilderness, a time in which people work out the significance of covenant. Those freshly covenanted will, like Israel in Moses' absence, be initially guided by images dominant in their past, even if they are motivated by the wonderful experience of deliverance. Those *in* con-formation may not be affected in their hearts, even if their heads are "properly" instructed. We need to internalize identity as members of God's people in this community; leaders need to give direction without domination or capitulation.

The enrollment into public ministry of adult, committed believers, is akin to the Shechem covenant. In re-formation, members learn to re-present God as known in their community in language, worlds, in situations hostile or alien to their own formation or con-formation. All who have internalized corporate identity through testing and disciplined obedience are called to re-embody, to incarnate and relinquish or avail to others in public mission and ministry their inheritance. Discerning how to re-present God in terms alien to us is a life-long process. Nurture and discipline are necessary foundations of ministry as God's servant.

The task of leaders in re-formation is to engage the diverse experiences all have had, to inquire into their significance, to relate together communal confrontation, correction and celebration. In this terrain the community re-forms the shape of its understanding in order to best serve God in this time and place. That entails asking how to nurture others whose story, worship, and liturgy differs from ours. We seek how to nurture and discipline belonging, and how to faithfully engage discipleship and commitment in experiences or formations other than our own. We inquire what theologies and practices best re-present God's love and life for people in various contexts in this day, in and as their inheritance as God's people.

The Church of Jesus Christ is the incarnate body of Jesus Christ. We are called to lifelong pilgrimage including nurture and formation, discipline and conformational testing, and interdependent service of God with one another as one Church in ministry and mission. It is intolerable that Christians be separated from other members of Jesus Christ. Separated Christians are amputees. Like Israel and Moses before God, we are covenanted together in Jesus Christ, but we are still in the wilderness. The unity promised us is threatened so long as each remembers and celebrates the icons of our formation in Jesus' name. We must bring the images of our particular inheritances to our common pilgrimage to God's promised fullness. Yet we choose daily whether to offer those images as norms for all to follow and then be astonished when God's covenant tablets are broken at our feet, or whether to relinquish our particular heritage as did Jesus, who "emptied himself. . .and became obedient unto death. . . ." (Phil. 2:7-8).

When humankind seems threatened by divine wrath, it is shielded by the tenacious ministries of those who hold to God and God's people. Wrath threatens to consume the future of God's creation and of God's incarnate body. Bold compassion calls all who belong to God to stand as Moses: together with God and with God's threatened people. Christians are called to relinquish whatever icons of faith divide rather than relate us in God's glorious covenant in Jesus Christ, who is our heritage and future as children of God. So long as Christians see our own frontsides and others' backsides, we will not move from this wilderness place. But inasmuch as we also confess our backsides, we may become one in God: who gives us promise, and who is our life, our hope, and our inheritance.

Christian Baptism:
The Evangelical Imperative

JEFFREY GROS, F.S.C.

Director, Commission on Faith and Order
National Council of the Churches of Christ

In reflecting on the course of this conference where we have reviewed the diversity within the believers' church of its own understandings of baptism and church membership and their relations, and the text of "Baptism" from the B.E.M. statement of the Commission on Faith and Order of the World Council of Churches, a clear evangelical imperative has emerged. Each of us believers' churches and pedobaptist churches, in sharing a faith in Jesus Christ and some relationship to the baptismal mandate of the Scriptures in our differences carry an imperative to ecumenical dialogue. My remarks in this section will focus not on the evangelical understanding of baptism, nor on baptism as a resource for evangelism. Rather, I will focus on the context for living out the evangelical witness of baptism today, which I am convinced we share. Secondly, I will discuss in some detail the imperative toward ecumenical dialogue.

I am most grateful as an outsider to be invited to participate in these conversations. Having grown up in a Roman Catholic minority among an "established" believers' church community in Memphis, where Roman Catholics, Orthodox, and some pedobaptist Christians were indeed a gathered and confessing minority within a context where the political and social life of the community, and the religious expectations were that of the Baptist churches, I understand very well what it is to carry a peculiar heritage in a minority situation. Likewise, I am not unsympathetic to the images some of your churches use from Daniel 8 and Revelation relative to elements in my own tradition. The beast and whore of Babylon imagery is certainly pre-Reformation and not unrelated to even your own understandings of the institutional elements in the church when in tension with the dynamic, charismatic element. I have no problem with the tiarad beasts of Daniel being used in Christian education, as long as those images are equally shared with distorted leadership dynamics, and the curial powers of one's own tradition.

Likewise, I am grateful as a staff person of the National Council of Churches to be part of this conference which I consider at the very center of the Faith and Order movement, bringing together disparate elements of the Christian community whose differences in faith and church order have not yet been reconciled, but seeking in Christ and the Scriptures modes of sharing and healing which will bring us closer to the evangelical imperative calling us to deeper unity. The diversity of the seven presentations, and other traditions unrepresented in those presentations, not only over baptism but over church order, discipline, peace witness, and other elements of church life point to the very same method and faith that is at the core of the Faith and Order movement. So while I come gratefully as an outsider to your midst as a Roman Catholic and as a member of the National Council staff, I feel very much the experience and spirituality of the believers' church as an influence in my own journey.

I.

Of the two points which provide the context and content of this discussion, the first is religious liberty. Let me say categorically that I agree with John Howard Yoder's assessment of the present situation and the search of responsible Christians, Orthodox, Catholic, and Protestant, to receive the testimony of the gathered believers in a world which has become hostile and secularist. Not only do we need to understand what it means to be a disestablished church in matters ecclesiastical, but also to be sensitive to the communal economic and peacemaking spiritual disciplines which are at the heart of the identity of some of your communions. We are all faced with being a minority consumed by a civil ethic which stands against an integral gospel humanism.

In this, speaking from my own tradition as a Roman Catholic, we have especially learned from the free church traditions in the United States context. You may know that history, but for those for whom it is not fresh, let me recount it briefly.[1]

In the late nineteenth century the Cardinal Archbishop of Baltimore, James Gibbons, in his dealings with the Vatican under Pope Leo XIII, had a great influence on the labor teaching of the Roman Catholic Church. This eventually gave rise to an encyclical on labor, *Rerum Novarum*, which is seen as the headwaters for contemporary styles of Roman Catholic social ethics, a church speaking freely within a free society. In the same period, John Ireland, Archbishop of St. Paul, became an advocate for the freedom of religion and separation of church and state as an ideal, not only for American Catholic Christians, but also for the old world churches of Europe. While the social ethical style of American Catholicism had a tremendous influence in the late nineteenth century, the ideal of separation of church and state, religious liberty, and pluralism was not so well received in the old world. In fact it evoked a Roman condemnation of "Americanism" in 1899, and with a reaction against Roman Catholic modernism under Pius X before the First World War, Roman Catholicism in the U.S. entered into a dark period of strong Romanism, intellectual timidity, and departure from the libertarian positions espoused by the leadership of the late nineteenth century.

To make a very long story short, these concerns within Roman Catholicism continued to percolate, however, and rose to the highest level of Roman Catholic discussion in the 1950s with their vindication at the Second Vatican Council in 1964 with the approval by the Council Fathers of the decree on religious liberty *Dignitatis Humanae* drafted by John Courtney Murray, and supported by Cardinals Meyer of Chicago and Ritter of St. Louis and Archbishop Montini, then of Milan. One would have to say explicitly at this point that the Roman Catholic confessional position on religious liberty is rooted in the American experience as Murray subtitles his book.[2]

To be honest, one must recognize very squarely that the American experience on which Murray is reflecting is embodied in the constitutional Bill of Rights given to our country from the Virginia Baptists, Southern Baptists, and therefore our Roman Catholic response to the evangelical insight about religious liberty must be laid at the feet of our Baptist Christian brethren. I think it is important for us to recognize, however, that we are not learning from the Baptists as Baptists, but rather as Christians who point us to a biblical insight which we as Roman Catholics have only gradually learned to share.

The key elements of *Dignitatis Humanae*[3] are: (1) religious liberty is rooted in human dignity, not merely a toleration of error; (2) a preference for constitutional government; and (3) the implications for toleration and pluralism in the secular order. Now while in voting on these documents the fathers of the Council are affirming the social ethic, it is quite clear that these three principles are being gradually applied within our own ecclesiastical life and ecclesiology.

For example, the question of liberty of conscience has had a tremendous impact on our own sacramental practice as witnessed by the intervention of Archbishop Roach on the sacrament of penance at the Synod in the fall of 1981[4]. Likewise, the preference for constitutional government in the civil order has constitutional ramifications for the revisions of Canon Law within Roman Catholicism,[5] and the desires for greater checks and balances, due process, and other Anglo-American styles of decision-making within Roman Catholic internal relations. Will we ever see a constitutionalized papacy or a separation of powers at the level of the episcopacy? It is hard to say, and the ecumenical dialogue will not be irrelevant in this matter. Thirdly, the focus on liberty has been influential in recapturing the biblical liberation insights which have been so important in some third world theologies. The multiplicity of tensions within Roman Catholicism which you read about today are a celebration of the Roman Catholic Church's willingness to struggle with believers' church values within its own life. One would invite the believers' churches to help us with this struggle, and recognize the creativity and evangelical reality of this tension.

As one author in the Southern Baptist/Roman Catholic dialogue has commented:

> Religious liberty which once seemed to mean the right of people to choose their religious allegiance, increasingly seems to mean as well the right of people to determine the degree and quality of their affiliation with any particular church. What this means is that American Catholic churches now face problems long faced by their Protestant counterparts: how to persuade people to select the Catholic communion over another, and at the same time impose a dogmatic and

moral discipline on members who are there because
they have freely chosen to be there. The challenge is
indeed awesome. It requires all Catholics to participate fully in the task of articulating belief, evangeliz-
ing themselves and those outside, and mutually cor-
recting and challenging one another. This offers a
road to a new and fuller unity based on free consent; it
also opens the door to partisan debate and division,
perhaps to the extent of multiplying diverse Catholic
communities, differing in style and belief as much as
Episcopalians differ from Baptists and AME Zion
churches differ from the Lutheran or Pentecostal. Pre-
serving and developing both unity and vitality in the
church is thus the great challenge of the next period of
American history.[6]

In the vein of the nineteenth-century debates between
Campbell and Purcell, one could say that Campbell won
and Roman Catholics have capitulated to the American
way, having taught to their universal communion of believers the principles of American separation of church and
state, an affirmation of individual conscience and upholding the inner working of the Spirit—and in addition—
moving to the traditional understanding of adult, believers
baptism as normative in their tradition. On the other hand,
one could say Purcell and the Roman Catholics have won
over Campbell in that they have survived as a minority,
albeit often persecuted in the dominant Protestant culture,
as good, loyal, and productive citizens, providing even-
handed public servants all the way to the highest office of the
land, with no hint of attempt to subvert the republic. They
of course see themselves as disenfranchised as conservative
evangelicals, believers' churches and recently dethroned
mainline Protestant establishments in a predominantly sec-

ular society where their own church membership is often
more informed by civil religion, than by the social ethic of
their tradition.

A final note, one need only recognize that after the
experience of Hitler and the Barmen Declaration alluded to
by John Howard Yoder, there is a chastened Christianity
seeing itself as believers amidst secularized culture. Catholicism, even minority papalist Catholicism since 1870–
1927–1964 and Spanish, anti-papal but state, Catholicism
since the demise of Franco in Spain and Medellin (1968) and
Puebla (1979) in Latin America, is also in this context. Since
its subjugation under Islam and final demise of any Con-
stantinian pretensions since 1917 in Russia, Eastern Orthodoxy is struggling with this same new situation which the
Anabaptists have lived with since the Reformation and the
Oriental Orthodox since the fifth and seventh centuries.

Therefore, we are all humbly in a position of learning
from the witness of the gathered churches where faith and
koinonia, not societal legitimation or control, are the foundation of our commitments—even commitments to particular ecclesiological and sacramental understandings. We
need to continue to find ways of working and believing
together to support those who "want to be Christians in
earnest and who profess the gospel with hand in mouth."[7]

II.

For my second major point, I would like to commence
by expressing appreciation to the comments of Hugh Bar-
bour, Quaker, for outlining an ecclesiology shared by Quakers and Roman Catholics, which leaves us with a common
sacramental understanding, though quite different practices! The biblical view which he articulated is that Jesus
Christ is the sacrament of the encounter with God, the
mysterion of Ephesians 4:32. The secondary sacrament of

God, the body of Christ, the church then is only a derivative sacrament/mystery, and in a sacramentalist understanding (and here is where we differ most from the Quakers) it is only in this context that faithful communities of believers embodying Jesus Christ can then speak of acts which participate in the mystery character, the graced reality. Thus, with the Quakers, Catholic theology would understand baptism as the act of that believing church which both discloses and obscures the transcendence of God in Christ in the believing community. Unlike Quakers, we are impelled to practice these signs, these sacraments, as feeble instruments of signifying and celebrating God's grace in our midst.

With that said, let me proceed to lay out the evangelical imperative and the quest for a common understanding of the Christian faith of which baptism is a key element. In this section, I would like to hold up five points for your consideration: (1) a way of understanding the imperative for the unity of the church, (2) others who are responding to the "Baptism" section of B.E.M. in ways that should call forth the witness of the believers' church, (3) further ecumenical resources in the discussion of baptism which might be of importance to the believers' church discussion, (4) the overall project of Faith and Order and where B.E.M. fits into that, and (5) some debates going on in the ecumenical movement that have an impact on those Christians seeking to be evangelical.

In affirming ecumenism at the center of the evangelical quest to which we are called by baptism and in which baptism is an integral element, I would only reinforce the remarks of Michael Kinnamon and contrast them with those of Lewis Mudge. That is, it seems to me, that the evangelical imperative of the unity of the church is grounded in a biblical doctrine of the Church articulated in 1 Corinthians 1, Acts 15, John 17, and Ephesians 4. Indeed we are called to be one for the sake of mission, yes, that the world might believe. However, we are called by the one Lord, father of Jesus Christ, to be those who serve the one church that the reality of the gospel might be revealed. The quest for the unity of the church is the quest for Jesus Christ at the center and the church as an expression of his healing and reconciling body on earth. This is a pilgrimage of believers toward truth and not a negotiated, much less manipulated, chess or football match.

If you are able to convince me or my church as Roman Catholic of the biblical judgment on my formulation or practice, indeed it can be a moment of renewal or even reconsideration for us. If however, new sociological and psychological formulations are produced, do not be surprised should I be more skeptical about forgoing traditional formulations or practices which at this point seem to be quite evangelical and biblically grounded.

Likewise, understandings and practices attested to among the believers' churches here present may in fact show at one point or another, greater evangelical and theological affinities for some churches who practice infant baptism. That is, our biblical understandings separate us along different lines depending on how we are talking about the action of the Spirit in baptism, the regenerative dimension of baptism, the relationship of immersion and pouring as adequate signs of the biblical witness, the dynamics of grace, the role of the ministry of the church in the process, the understanding of the meaning of faith and familial community support, and innumerable other points of our faith. Such recognition of the diversity, and the tentative character of the biblical witness, should not lead us to a simple relativism which seems to be the confessional stand of some in the Christian community.[8] Indeed, the recognition of diversity and the willingness to deal with ambiguity in the ecumenical movement should not be a call to relativism, while it does call us to humility before the truth of the gospel calling us toward unity.

At this point, I think it is important to lay out what I would consider four complementary elements in the movement toward Christian unity which are indeed diverse, some of which like your own would not carry the title "ecumenical," or appreciate being associated with the institutions of the ecumenical movement:

(1) There are those grass roots informal dialogues or affinity groups in churches, like this conference, that gather in order to probe the gospel as it relates to their own internal diversity and bring about a greater level of reconciliation. Certainly evangelicalism is an ecumenical movement in this sense, as are such organizations as the Society for Pentecostal Studies, the Wesleyan Theological Society, and the Evangelical Theological Society. In each the gospel truth contributes to the unity of the church, whatever the self-definition of these ecumenical processes.[9]

(2) There is the world-wide Faith and Order movement, which finds fragile institutional expression within the World Council of Churches and the National Council of Churches, which is working on themes of Scripture and tradition at Montreal (1963) and other projects. I would recommend to you in this context the Louisville Consultation alluded to by Michael Kinnamon which indeed was an attempt to bring together believers' baptist churches with others to have direct impact on this particular document.[10]

(3) The bilateral conversations going on between pairs of churches attempting, with Scripture and the common study of history, to work through historic divergences using the Faith and Order methodology. I would recommend to you particularly the Baptist/Lutheran dialogue and the Southern Baptist/Roman Catholic scholars' dialogue. Likewise I would suggest that you follow the worldwide Baptist/

Catholic dialogue which will begin this summer at a meeting in Berlin.[11] You will be interested to know that the Roman Catholic/Orthodox bilateral dialogue meeting in June, 1983 on Crete discussed these same questions of initiation, issues which are seen by these two communions still to divide them among themselves and not only from the believers' churches.

(4) Church union movements which have incorporated believers' churches are an important set of experiences for reflecting on believers' churches in the evangelical call to unity. The role of the Christian Church (Disciples of Christ) in the Consultation on Church Union is particularly interesting to those open to the convergences of baptism in B.E.M. The Louisville Faith and Order consultation has some reflections on the churches of North India and Pakistan which are union churches including believers' and infant baptism options with all of the attendant theological and pastoral problems. Therefore, there are learnings for us, not only from one another in our still divided situation, but also from churches which have restored the fellowship while honoring the consciences of both traditions.

In looking at the text of your response, and listening to the discussions, one fears that the ecumenical movement moves forward without the testimony of the believers' churches. I would like to witness to the fact that those in sacramental churches feel as though the ecclesiology and the understanding of their church has been totally by-passed in this document as well, and that there are responses already emerging, which give the impression that the believers' churches have controlled the outcome of the document. As was quite clear from the Kinnamon presentation, the Faith and Order methodology, in fact, in looking for the gospel truth with an honest appraisal of where we are with one another is what the text is about. However, it is important to recognize that there is a possibility of learning from one another and to see the B.E.M. document as an opportunity to engage, even in difference, over a common element of our faith. As Mudge indicated, this fragile bridge of words will indeed heighten our tensions as we know one another better. The tension will take place within our mutual respect and understanding of one another as Christian.

The believers' churches need to find ways of hearing the concerns about individual, consumer-voluntarism and post-enlightenment (possibly non-biblical) understandings of faith that are seen by others in the believers' churches and in the document. It is only the presence of believers' church persons embodying the witness of these traditions which can allay the stereotypes of other churches, and point to the evangelical content of their faith. As examples of these responses let me lift up two. The third draft of the United Methodist theologians' response prepared on the baptismal document begins a long section by saying:

> . . . This is all true [No. 12] from the standpoint of psychology and baptismal practice. However, the implication is that infant baptism is not as complete a rite as the baptism of adults. We find this theologically questionable. We believe the ecumenical movement will need to pay more attention to the theological foundations of infant baptism and give stronger emphasis to the corporate and communal understanding of faith.[12]

This draft which will be revised at least twice more before publication, goes on to include five more paragraphs on why this seems to be essential to the biblical faith.

Or another, this time a private—but seasoned—Roman Catholic ecumenist responds:

Underlying the modern difference, however, there is a different understanding of faith rather than of baptism.

If faith is understood as a personal response to the preaching of the gospel as it is attested in Scripture, then it is obvious that infants cannot be said to share faith. And this is the origin of the reluctance to baptize them. It is an understanding of faith which, if pressed to the exclusion of wider considerations, eventually robs baptism of its significance: it is in danger of becoming an optional extra for those who are saved and justified by their personal confession of faith, a ritual carried out because it is dictated by Scripture and tradition, but only as a vivid symbolic demonstration of what has been effected already.

If, however, one understands faith as basically a recognition of and response to Christ dwelling and living in Christian persons, i.e., the church, then a justification for baptizing the children of Christian parents emerges. A child meets the forestalling love of God in his mother's love. In the Christian family he learns bit by bit to discover the Christian content of this global experience of love. . . . An infant recently born has already entered on the process of becoming a person, and there are no definable leaps or breaks in the growth of a Christian person in a Christian community: it goes on all our lives.

So, we all hold by believers' baptism. Where we differ is in our understanding of faith.[13]

While these two examples do not produce new arguments, they point to the new levels of engagement which we can celebrate and into which we can draw our laity and leadership as a moment of reconciliation, even in the tensions of honest differences over the gospel of Jesus Christ.

III.

As a third point in the discussion of the evangelical imperative to the unity of the church, I would like to lay out the broader context of the Faith and Order studies to flesh out what Mudge and Kinnamon have said. It seems apparent in the discussion and drafting of the report that it would be useful to see the other elements besides B.E.M. As Michael Kinnamon and John Howard Yoder have reminded us, the shifts in the Faith and Order movement to a Christ-centered, common biblical and historical method have been characteristic of the last two or three decades of the Faith and Order movement producing what scholars, Protestant, Catholic, and Orthodox, felt was an adequate agreement on the authority of sacred Scripture and the understanding of tradition. It is clear that a reappraisal of this convergence will be necessary for some before the subsequent work will have relevance. I can assure you from the experience of the Standing Commission on Faith and Order meeting in Crete, in April, 1984, that the leadership of the commission is quite aware that in the first responses to B.E.M. it will become necessary to clarify again Faith and Order's understanding of the relationship of Scripture and tradition and possibly re-publish and re-distribute this previous work. It may stand the test of time and be an adequate understanding to which you as believers' churches and others can attest as a basis of authority of Scripture on which to move, or it may require further dialogue, discussion, and convergence.

Since the discussions of Scripture and tradition in Montreal in 1963, Faith and Order has produced major reflections on the nature of the unity we seek, "in each place and in every place." In a study produced in 1973 and incorporated into the work of the Nairobi Assembly of the World Council in 1975, a vision of conciliar fellowship was held up before the churches.[14] This study lays out the hope for church unity based on councils of churches, theologically understood by Protestant, Orthodox, and Catholic, in continuity with that described in Acts 15 of the apostles, and related, in those churches for whom this is of relevance, to the early councils of Nicea (325) and Constantinople (381). Such councils could only meet were the truth of the gospel agreed upon in such a way that three elements would be realized—a common understanding of: (1) recognition of one another's baptism, eucharist, and ministry; (2) common expression of the one apostolic/biblical faith; and (3) having common ways of deciding and acting together.

When questions are raised about the 1982 B.E.M. document, it is important to realize this wider context of the Faith and Order program and that B.E.M. is not being discussed without having had previous discussions on the nature of the church and its unity and the authority of Scripture and tradition. Likewise it is important to recognize that the level of doctrinal consensus and the question of church order and church authority are on the agenda, though for the future. B.E.M., then, is only one element in a long pilgrimage of theological discussion creating bases on which the churches can become more reconciled. However, while B.E.M. is in the process of reception, it is necessary to keep the hope for conciliar fellowship in the background and to recognize that these other research projects are in process.

"Toward a Common Expression of the Apostolic Faith Today" is just beginning. It is a project in which the National Council as well as the World Council is involved and in which members of this group are participants. In the

National Council it is a project headed up by a member of a believers' church, Glenn Hinson, a Southern Baptist. It would be important that the Believers' Church Conference take this topic most seriously and see that its witness, as churches largely non-creedal, have their appropriate witness.[15]

As well as one needs to recognize that Scripture and tradition have been discussed, that the vision of the church as conciliar fellowship is a backdrop for B.E.M., and that a study of the Apostolic Faith is underway, it is also important to recognize that the authority question is not being skirted. The project on deciding and acting together, authority, is years away from beginning, though it is expected that the B.E.M. reception process will disclose to the Faith and Order movement as well as the churches to one another, a rich diversity of church orders and theological understandings of authority which will again be available as the theological discussions commence eventually on deciding and acting together. There were those who would have liked, for example, questions of a Petrine ministry to be introduced in the ministry section of B.E.M. However, there were many voices, Roman Catholic among them, who felt as though the question of the papacy was not indeed a ministry question from the evangelical perspective, but one of authority. Of course there are many—both Roman Catholic and other—who feel as though the papacy is not an evangelical question at all, but indeed it is part of the unity discussions and must be addressed eventually, as it has already been addressed in some of the bilateral conversations.[16]

Fourthly, in talking about the bilateral conversations, I would like to single out particularly the usefulness of the Lutheran/Baptist discussions because they focus on the very important areas of the theology of the child which have been a major discussion in this consultation. This discussion of the theology of the child is set within the context, not only of baptism as a rite, but the questions of faith, understood in the New Testament, and grace, so important in the Lutheran contributions to all of the Reformation churches. In this context I would also encourage looking at the Lutheran/Catholic development on justification, as a wider context in which reformation discussions, of which all western churches are heirs, are moving towards resolution.[17] In some ways these discussions on our understanding of God's action in history and the role of modern methods of biblical study are just beginning. The challenges to our traditional anthropologies by psychology, sociology, and the secular discipline of anthropology are also important. One will have to judge for oneself the extent to which the christology and soteriology lying behind the doctrines of grace and faith in the Reformation debates are being resolved. However, all of this is at the very heart of the believers' church discussion, and provides the larger context in which baptism is being reviewed by our churches.

Finally, a brief note on the evangelical imperative as it touches those who take to themselves the name "evangelical" in our culture. That is, Christians, some of your constituents among them, whose sensitivities move towards the National Association of Evangelicals and the publication, *Christianity Today*. While many of you will not find this to be your own area of discussion, I find it an irony that in your draft response there is not the boldness to urge upon your constituencies a reconsideration of relationships with the conciliar movement on the one hand, and deep knowledge of the documents that have been produced by the ecumenical movement on the other. In a recent editorial in *Christianity Today* we find just the opposite—that is, an urging upon the evangelical constituency a reconsideration of its relationship to the ecumenical movement on the one hand, and a demonstrated lack of penetration of the theological contents of the documents emerging therefrom. While this discussion, might I say ecumenical dialogue, within the community calling itself "evangelical" may not be of relevance to you, it is part of the reconciling agenda of all who would confess Jesus Christ in search for the biblical unity of the church as part of their evangelical imperative.

As some of your may know, after the Vancouver Assembly of the World Council, a serious article appeared in *Christianity Today* by Richard Lovelace, praising the evangelical import of Vancouver and encouraging those who have separated themselves from the conciliar movement to reconsider that decision.[18] That article drew forth significant debate within the evangelical community, including strong criticism of Lovelace's point of view and calls to evangelicals to continue to witness against the conciliar movement.

The April 20, 1984 edition of *Christianity Today* produced an editorial as carefully drafted as the paper you have done or any World Council document, an ecumenical enterprise as skillfully produced as any emerging from the Roman curia. In it there is the recommendation:

> How, then, shall evangelicals respond to the new winds stirring in the World Council? We certainly cannot speak for all evangelicals. Recognizing that some may chart quite a different course, we for our part commend the following approach:
>
> 1. *Listen* to hear what the WCC is really saying. . . .
> 2. *Dialogue* from a position of faith. The evangelical is not searching for the gospel; by grace he has heard and received it. To some, this may sound arrogant. To the evangelical, this is his assurance of faith in the truth and goodness of God.

> 3. *But still he must dialogue.*
> 4. *Pray.*
> 5. *Love.*

> Yet, so long as the World Council fails to teach essential truth, or in its teaching and practice denies what is essential to biblical Christianity, we shall continue to oppose it, and to warn against its subversion of the faith. And though other evangelicals may disagree, we shall refuse to support it or identify with it.[19]

If there appears to be a contradiction here between a recommendation to dialogue listening, prayer, and love on the one hand and a refusal to support on the other, in fact, it is the characteristic of a true ecumenical convergence statement to incorporate the diversity of points of view within a particular community. Indeed, it is encouraging to see the deep ecumenical commitment which the *Christianity Today* editorial staff has to the World Council. One wonders whether the identity of this community would be quite so clear without the gift of the World Council as an element in the dialogue.

Another factor in this editorial which is fascinating is the discussion emanating from the criticism of one of the speakers at Vancouver:

> We are not asking the World Council to clear up all the mysteries of the eternal trinity or to unravel how the human and divine natures are related to each other in the one person of Jesus of Nazareth. Yet we are asking the Council to stop giving mere lip service to an undefined doctrine of the deity of Christ that permits it to teach anything. In short, the World Council must clean up its act. It must let us hear a consistent

commitment to a basic Nicean and Chalcedonian
christology, for this is the very heart of biblical
revelation.[20]

It is quite clear that this is a response to a particular
speaker at Vancouver, carefully selected out of the dozens of
orthodox voices in order to prove a polemic point. One
wonders whether the careful work on Nicene and Chalcedonian christology is being hidden from the readership of
Christianity Today or the authors of the editorial are merely
ignorant of these documents.[21] It is interesting to raise the
question of how "free" are the free churches and how "non-
confessional" are the believers' churches' voices who contribute to the "evangelical" perspective in our American
culture. Though these questions may not be of specific
import to any individuals of your constituency, they are part
of the interplay of Christians in our community in ways that
draw us together in discussing the common evangelical
imperative celebrated in our diverse baptism, testifying to
faith in one Christ that challenges us to find the unity of the
church.

SECTION III:
Believers' Baptism and the Meaning of Church Membership

A Reception Response Statement

A non-ecclesial "reception" response to the "Baptism" section of the "Baptism, Eucharist, and Ministry" document produced and circulated by the Faith and Order Commission of the World Council of Churches.

by

The Seventh Conference on the Believers' Church
convening on the campus
of Anderson School of Theology
Anderson, Indiana, USA
June 5–8, 1984

CONTEXT

For many persons in the several Christian churches in North America which practice "believers' baptism" rather than baptizing infants, the appearance of the "Baptism, Eucharist, and Ministry" document has evoked considerable interest—particularly the section on baptism. They quickly note the fact that, along with pedobaptism, recognition is given to the believers' baptism position as an aspect of authentic Christian practice.

Several such persons in conversation and correspondence expressed a desire to study this document more thoroughly, but, since many were associated with communions which are not members of the World Council of Churches, they would not likely have the opportunity to do so in a corporate setting. Most of these interested people, however, had participated in one or more earlier conferences dealing with various aspects of "The Concept of the Believers' Church," so it occurred to some that this might be a possible vehicle for doing such an exercise. And, since the WCC's Faith and Order Commission had specifically asked for responses to the reception of the document, it seemed appropriate, and hopefully profitable, that this interdenominational cluster of academicians and church leaders give their collective attention at least to the "Baptism" section of the B.E.M. statement and prepare their own reception response. The Believers' Church Conference's committee on continuing conversations concurred. Accordingly this seventh Conference was planned by an *ad hoc* committee and was convened in early June, 1984, being hosted by Anderson School of Theology and co-sponsored by three other seminaries: Associated Mennonite Biblical Seminaries, Bethany Theological Seminary, and Christian Theological Seminary.

It is obvious that this conference had no ecclesial status. Participation was voluntary. Those present were there as interested persons, not officially designated representatives of their various communions. The constituency of the conference, however, was broadly representative with more than sixty participants coming from fifteen different communions. Some of the most widely known scholars from several of these churches were present. To provide adequate background for understanding all the issues the program included addresses by the secretary of the drafting committee for the B.E.M. document, a former executive of WCC's Faith and Order Commission, and a staunch defender of pedobaptism. The main work of the conference, however, was in small groups which assessed the "Baptism" statement line by line.

Conferees were unanimous in expressing overall appreciation for the thoroughness and quality of the document and for the extensive process of reception which the Commission suggests. In order to make the response of this conference comparable with others the four point outline suggested in the preface to the B.E.M. document was followed. The drafting process was intendedly decentralized, more to provoke interaction than to produce a polished text. The final editing was done after the meeting. This edited version presupposes the reader would have an available B.E.M. text for reference.

PREFACE

We have heard concerns expressed by participants from several "believers' church" groups. Out of that context we have begun to consider whether the "Baptism" text of B.E.M. represents "the faith of the church." We appreciate the opportunity to respond to the document.

RESPONSE

I. The extent to which we recognize in this text the apostolic faith of the church . . .
   A. We recognize the following elements as being a part of that faith:
      1. The extensive use of biblical vocabulary and imagery, particularly in paragraph 1–10. The composition process obviously did not begin with "hardened" creeds but rather with Scripture. Yet, beginning with paragraph 11 the biblical references cease.

2. The affirmation that "baptism is both God's gift and our human response." (Paragraph 8)
3. The link between baptism and the Holy Spirit.
4. The administration of baptism in the name of the Father, Son, and Holy Spirit, according to Matthew 28.
5. The emphasis on baptism as participation in the life, death, and resurrection of Jesus Christ.
6. The link between baptism and incorporation into the church, although some of our churches do not identify baptism with church membership as closely as others.
7. The emphasis on a close relationship between baptism and ongoing nurture and growth in the Christian church.
8. The explicit integration of baptism and a new moral commitment, both personal and social.

B. We do, however, have difficulty recognizing the apostolic faith in the following areas:

1. The ambiguous and imperative language in Paragraph 13.

   We *agree* with paragraph 11 that the "most clearly attested pattern in the New Testament" is baptism upon personal confession of faith. We *disagree* among ourselves, however, in regard to the validity of infant baptism. Whereas some believers' churches do not accept infant baptism as baptism, they, without reservation, recognize as brothers and sisters in Christ those who confess Jesus as Lord and Savior. Some, in fact, would accept in their churches, upon profession of faith, persons baptized as infants, whereas others would require Believers' baptism, but would not regard such as "re-baptism."

2. The lack of a clear statement (section I & II) about the active role of the baptismal participant in making a public faith response and in identifying with the community of faith at the time of his or her baptism.

3. The lack of a close connection between baptism and the "ordination" of all believers to Christian ministry.

4. The lack of an express reference to church discipline as implied in the baptismal commitment.

5. The apparent identification of the sign of baptism with the reality signified, as for example, the sacramental language of paragraph 8: "the embodied . . . in baptism" and in paragraph 14, baptism "effects" participation in Christ's death and resurrection and reception of the Spirit.

6. The lack of definition or stated criteria for the phrase, "indiscriminate baptism" (Paragraph 16 and commentary on 21 b).

II. Consequences our churches can draw from B.E.M. for its relationships and dialogues with other churches . . .

A. The "Baptism" statement encourages us to see the views and practices of other churches in the light of their ecclesial life and history and their theological and confessional integrity, providing a helpful basis for conversation.

B. Our consideration of the B.E.M. document expresses acceptance of other traditions as Christian partners in dialogue.

III. The guidance our churches can take from this text:

A. B.E.M. stimulates us to think more deeply about our own theology of baptism.

B. The Study of the document requires believers' churches to examine how seriously they practice believers' baptism in regard to their own integrity and in dialogue with other churches.

C. The document is further instructive to us in believers' churches in the following ways:

1. In giving importance to reaffirming our own baptismal vows when others are baptized;
2. In reminding us that baptism is part of the corporate life of the church;
3. In reminding us of our corporate responsibility to nurture our children as they grow toward faith and baptism.

D. Consideration of issues raised by the "Baptism" statement in the light of the psychology of human development forces reconsideration of the appropriate age for a genuine believers' baptism.

IV. *Suggestions for the ongoing work of Faith & Order* . . .

A. We recommend that the long-range project, "Towards the Common Expression of the Apostolic Faith Today," continue to employ a broadly consultative process, including representation by individuals from various believers' churches.

B. We recommend for further study:

1. The items in I,B above.
2. Paragraph 19 of the B.E.M. document. It is by no means obvious to us that such "vivid signs" as are attested to by tradition but not by Scripture "may be expected to enrich the liturgy." Rather, the churches of our persuasion have moved toward simplicity and even austerity in worship.

3. A formulation of the ecclesiological, christological, and soteriological foundations and/or implications of baptismal practice.

4. A recognition that not "all" do in fact agree that Christian baptism is in water and the Holy Spirit (paragraph 14; Comm. 21c; cf. 11).

C. A consideration of the bearing upon the document of the following basic affirmation which we, as believers' churches, feel compelled to make:

1. We recognize that we share with all Christians a common confession of Jesus Christ as Lord and Saviour, according to the Scriptures.

2. We recognize that in finding Jesus Christ as the focus and norm of our commitment, we come to Scripture from given traditions.

3. Many of us would wish to add that Scripture is to be regarded as the sole source and criterion of Christian belief, standing as the authoritative corrective to our various traditions.

4. We would, therefore, urge that more explicit acknowledgment of the diverse views of Scripture and tradition be included—in particular, as representing the presuppositions of the section on baptism in the B.E.M. document.

5. We recognize the integrity of the particular baptismal traditions in their contexts, without at the same time accepting their universal validity.

Appendices

Random and Impressionistic Survey On Present Baptismal Teaching and Practices: A Checklist

1. The primary theological understanding of baptism, is it seen and taught as:

   a. participation in the cross and resurrection of Jesus Christ;

   b. a symbol of conversion, pardoning, and cleansing;

   c. a symbol of the gift of the Holy Spirit;

   d. a symbol of commitment to a life of discipleship;

   e. something else?

2. How does the congregation work with the whole matter of Christian nurture in relation to baptism (cf. paragraph 12 in the WCC "Baptism" document)?

3. Is there a teaching and/or practice of child dedication? Is this understood and practiced primarily as the blessing or dedication of children or as the dedication and commitment of parents?

4. Does the congregation and/or conference recommend or require "rebaptism" of those who may join Mennonite churches after having been baptized in pedobaptist churches?

5. How is the relation between water baptism and baptism of the Spirit understood?

6. What form of baptism is usually used?

7. What is the relationship between baptism and church membership?

8. Are there any trends in the average age at which children of Christian parents are baptized? Do people need to request baptism? Is there a regular instructional class after which young people are more or less "automatically" baptized?

THE CONFERENCES ON THE CONCEPT OF THE BELIEVERS' CHURCH
Themes and Reports

(1) The Concept of the Believers' Church; convened by Southern Baptist Seminary, at Louisville, KY. Coordinated by James Leo Garrett, Jr.; 26–30 June, 1967: report volume *The Concept of the Believers' Church* edited by James Leo Garrett, Jr., Scottdale, Herald Press, 1968.

(2) Is There a Christian Style of Life for Our Age?; convened by Chicago Theological Seminary at Chicago. Coordinated by Clyde L. Manschreck; 29 June–2 July, 1970: report in *Chicago Theological Seminary Register*, Vol. LX, No. 6, September 1970.

(3) Restitution, Dissent, and Renewal; convened by Pepperdine University, at Malibu, CA. Coordinated by Richard M. Hughes; report: *Journal of the American Academy of Religion*, Vol. XLIV, No. 1, March 1976.

(4) The Believers' Church, a conference for laity, convened by Laurelville Mennonite Church Center at Mount Pleasant, PA. Coordinated by Arnold Cressman, 26–29 May, 1972.

(5) The Believers' Church in Canada; convened by the Baptist Federation of Canada and the Mennonite Central Committee at Winnipeg, Man.; 15–18 May, 1978. Conference coordinated and report volume *The Believers' Church in Canada* edited by Jarold K. Zeman and Walter Klaassen. Report published 1979 by Baptist Federation of Canada and Mennonite Central Committee.

(6) Is There a Believers' Church Christology?; convened by Bluffton College at Bluffton, OH; 23–25 October, 1980. Coordinated by J. Denny Weaver.

(7) Believers' Baptism and the Meaning of Church Membership; sponsored by Anderson School of Theology, Associated Mennonite Biblical Seminaries, Bethany Theological Seminary, and Christian Theological Seminary and convened at Anderson, IN; 5–8 June, 1984. Coordinated by John W. V. Smith.

A Brethren-Friends-Mennonite consultation held 8–16 June, 1964 at Quaker Hill, Richmond, IN, counts in the memories of some as the beginning of the series. It was there that Franklin H. Littell presented his paper "The Historic Free Church Defined," *Brethren Life and Thought,* IX (Autumn 1964), 78–90; cf. also his "The Concerns of the Believers' Church," *Chicago Theological Seminary Register,* LVIII (December 1967), 18.

Report volumes are cited only where a specific book gathered most of the papers of a conference.

NOTES

Introduction

1. See Appendix B for the list of conferences and publications.

2. The classic typological synthesis is *The Believers' Church* by Donald Durnbaugh (New York: Macmillan, 1968; Scottdale, Pa.: Herald, 1985), but the typology was that of Max Weber, following up more objectively, formally the polemic notions of Gottfried Arnold (d. 1714) and Ludwig Keller (d. 1915). Professor Durnbaugh has been at the heart of the conference series since its beginning. He led the findings committee at Louisville and was one of the moderators at Anderson. Cf. Note 6 below.

3. A leading outside interpreter besides Weber and Williams is Franklin H. Littell, who prefers "Free Church."

4. Cf. Yoder, "The Nature of the Unity We Seek: A Historic Free Church View," in J. Robert Nelson, ed., *Christian Unity in North America* (St. Louis: Bethany, 1958), pp. 89-97; "The Free Church Ecumenical Style," in *Quaker Religious Thought*, 10:1 (Summer 1968):29-38.

5. Cf. the two Louisville summary documents, James Leo Garrett, Jr., ed., *The Concept of the Believers' Church* (Scottdale, Pa.: Herald, 1968), 314-23.

6. The way "restitution" sought in the nineteenth century to transcend denominationalism was a uniquely American possibility. Yet, since the Hussites, radical renewal has regularly included an ethos of dialogue, called "the rule of Christ" in the sixteenth century, implied by the rejection of civil coercion in matters of faith.

7. The Faith and Order Commission of the WCC has in recent years included individuals from communions not members of the WCC; thus, there was a strong Roman Catholic presence in the last years of the B.E.M. drafting.

Chapter 1

1. Lynn Miller, departmental assistant at AMBS, interviewed over twenty conference and congregational leaders in mid-western United States and in Ontario on the basis of a questionnaire which I prepared. See Appendix A.

2. John H. Yoder, *The Legacy of Michael Sattler* (Scottdale, Pa.: Herald, 1972), p. 36.

3. Ibid., p. 37.

4. Ibid.

5. See Rollin S. Armour, *Anabaptist Baptism: A Representative Study* (Scottdale, Pa.: Herald, 1966), pp. 46 ff.

6. Ibid., pp. 121ff.

7. In J. C. Wenger, ed., *Complete Writings of Menno Simons* (Scottdale, Pa.: Herald, 1974), pp. 103ff.

8. Ibid., pp. 227ff.

9. In Thieleman J. van Braght, *Martyr's Mirror* (Scottdale, Pa.: Mennonite Publishing House, 1951), pp. 38ff. The "Dordrecht Confession" has been printed, translated into German and English for use among North American Mennonites, frequently reprinted, and broadly used as a catechetical piece until very recently. Article VIII is on baptism.

10. "Christian Baptism," in Wenger, *Complete Writings*, p. 244.

11. See Armour, pp. 55, 95.

12. For example, see Gideon Yoder, *The Nurture and Evangelism of Children* (Scottdale, Pa.: Herald, 1959); more recently, see especially Marlin Jeschke, *Believers' Baptism for Children of the Church* (Scottdale, Pa.: Herald, 1983), and Maurice Martin and Helen Reusser, *In the Midst of the Congregation* (Scottdale, Pa.: Mennonite Publishing House, 1983).

13. J. Howard Kauffman and Leland Harder, *Anabaptists Four Centuries Later* (Scottdale, Pa.: Herald, 1975), p. 71.

14. See footnote 1.

Chapter 2

1. Alexander Mack, Jr., "Apologia," in Donald Durbaugh, ed., *The Brethren in Colonial America* (Elgin: Brethren Press, 1967), p. 510.

2. Marcus Barth, "Baptism and Evangelism," *Scottish Journal of Theology* 12 (March 1959); 40.

3. Minutes of the 194th Recorded *Annual Conference of the Church of Brethren*, Pittsburgh, Pennsylvania, June 24–29, 1980 (Elgin: Brethren Press, 1980), p. 95.

Chapter 3

1. Richard Bernard, *Plaine Evidences: The Church of England is Apostolicall, the Separation Schismaticall* (London, 1610), p. 17. Cf. Timothy George, "Between

Pacifism and Coercion: The English Baptist Doctrine of Religious Toleration," *Mennonite Quarterly Review* 58 (1984): 30–49.

2. Michael R. Watts, *The Dissenters* (Oxford: Clarendon, 1978), p. 66.

3. Article 40 of the *London Confession* in John H. Leith, ed., *Creeds of the Churches* (Atlanta: John Knox, 1982), p. 719.

4. Thomas Edwards, *Gangraena* (London, 1646), Pt. i, p. 204.

5. Cf. the excellent study by William L. Lumpkin, *Baptist Foundations in the South* (Nashville: Broadman, 1961).

6. A. C. Dayton, *Theodosia Ernest; or, The Heroine of Faith* (1856; Philadelphia: American Baptist Publication Society, 1903), pp. 3–4. A Methodist response was written by William P. Harrison: *Theophilus Walton; or, The Majesty of Truth* (Nashville: Stevenson and Owen, 1858).

7. I follow here the distinctions outlined by E. Glenn Hinson, "Baptism and Christian Unity: A Baptist Perspective," in George A. Kilcourse, ed., *Baptism: An Ecumenical Starting Point* (Lexington, Ky.: Kentucky Council of Churches, 1982), pp. 20–30.

Chapter 4A

1. Cf. the following major historical accounts of the Church of God: A. L. Byers, *Birth of a Reformation; or, The Life of D. S. Warner* (Anderson: Gospel Trumpet, 1921); Charles Ewing Brown, *When the Trumpet Sounded* (Anderson: Warner, 1951); and John W. V. Smith's commemorative centennial volume, *The Quest for Holiness and Unity* (Anderson: Warner, 1980).

2. Sarah Smith, *Life Sketches of Mother Sarah Smith* (Guthrie, Okl.: Faith Publishing House, n.d.), pp. 28–29.

3. D. S. Warner, *The Church of God: And What the Church Is Not* (Anderson: Warner, n.d.), pp.6–7.

4. D. S. Warner, *Salvation: Present, Perfect, Now or Never* (Anderson: Gospel Trumpet, n.d.), pp. 17–20.

5. R. R. Byrum, *Christian Theology* (Anderson: Gospel Trumpet, 1925), p. 518.

6. Ibid., p. 515.

7. H. M. Riggle, *The New Testament Church: Spiritual, Practical* (Anderson: Gospel Trumpet, 1937), p. 126.

8. F. G. Smith, *What the Bible Teaches*, rev. ed. (Anderson: Gospel Trumpet, 1945), p. 168. Cf. A. F. Gray, *Christian Theology*, 2 vols. (Anderson: Warner, 1946), 2:115–17.

9. F. G. Smith, *What the Bible Teaches*, p. 168; and Riggle, *New Testament Church*, pp. 126–28.

10. C. E. Brown, *The Church Beyond Division* (Anderson: Gospel Trumpet, 1939), p. 128. As Brown (p. 115) conceived the whole question of church membership: "Why should it be necessary to argue that human beings must be more exacting than is Christ, the head of the church? If Christ accepts a person into his church, knowing perfectly as he does the state of that person's heart, how can we be bold enough to say that a Christian may have satisfied the demands of the Lord but he has not satisfied ours? In other words, what is good enough for the heart-searching wisdom of God must be good enough for the humanity-dimmed eye of his children."

11. Earl W. Martin, *This We Believe . . . This We Proclaim* (Anderson: Gospel Trumpet, 1952), p. 75.

12. A. D. Khan, *Baptism* (Anderson: Gospel Trumpet, n.d.), pp. 5–6; cf. Smith, *What the Bible Teaches*, p. 188. H. M. Riggle's words are somewhat typical of this viewpoint: "In those early days [NT era] the minister led the candidate down into the water and baptized him; now the preacher stands on the dry floor of his beautiful meeting house. At that time the people were buried in baptism; now a few drops are sprinkled on the hair or snapped in the face. In some of the more stylish places the hats of the proud ladies are not even removed, and only their feathers and flowers receive the sprinkles. In primitive times, after baptism, people came up out of the water; now they walk on the soft carpet to their seats. Oh, how changed! Truly the apostasy has made void the commandments of God and substituted traditions instead" (*Christian Baptism, the Lord's Supper, and Feetwashing* [Anderson: Gospel Trumpet, 1909], p. 29). Even after other rationales were accepted for the movement's purpose, infant baptism has been regarded as emblematic of a less than vital Christianity; see Gray, *Christian Theology*, 2:150; and Brown, *We Preach Christ: A Handbook of Christian Doctrine* (Anderson: Gospel Trumpet, 1957), p. 125.

13. Byrum, *Christian Theology*, pp. 570–71; Gray, *Christian Theology*, 2:149–50; Brown, *Church Beyond Division*, p. 115; Khan, *Baptism*, p. 22; Hillery C. Rice, *"And Be Baptized"* (Anderson: n.p., n.d.), pp. 15–16; Herschell D. Rice, *The Truth About Baptism* (Anderson: Gospel Trumpet, n.d.) n.p.; Riggle, *Christian Baptism*, pp. 76–84.

14. Riggle, *Christian Baptism*, p. 21. Cf. E. E. Byrum, *The Ordinances of the Bible* (Moundsville, W. Va.: Gospel Trumpet, 1903). Endorsers of immersion also specifically and vociferously repudiated trine immersion.

15. "Baptism is one of the commands necessary to obey in order that we may enjoy eternal salvation. Our future, eternal salvation is predicated upon faith in,

and obedience to, the whole gospel of Christ. This includes baptism as well as other rites and commands of the Savior. Mark 16:15, 16; Matt. 28:20. To willfully disregard it and set it aside is to be finally damned" (ibid., p. 110). See also a conclusion about the "early leaders," somewhat unwarranted, in Kenneth Eugene Renfrow, "Baptism: Theological, Institutional and Contemporary," unpublished B. D. thesis, Anderson School of Theology, 1960.

16. In cases where those baptized as infants had come to mature confessions of faith and in the case of the restoration of persons who had fallen into "gross, public sin" and subsequently returned to the Christian life.

17. Riggle, *New Testament Church*, pp. 126–28; Martin, *This We Believe*, p. 80; Brown, *Church Beyond Division*, p. 115; Gray, *Christian Theology*, 2:148–49.

18. The figure of burial with Christ provided the late Dale Oldham with a common sense argument for immersion: ". . . You cannot bury a man by sprinkling dirt on his casket or by pouring a bucket of dirt on him. Paul said, 'We are buried with him by baptism.' Burial means burial, and it can mean nothing else." *Should You Be Baptized?* (Anderson: Gospel Trumpet, n.d.), n.p.

19. Hillery C. Rice, *Have You Been Baptized Since You Believed?* (Anderson: Gospel Trumpet, n.d.), p. 8; Byrum, *The Ordinances of the Bible*, pp. 50–51.

20. A. F. Gray, *Christian Theology*, 2:90–91; Byrum, *Christian Theology*, p. 575; A. L. Byers, *Baptism: Its Symbolism, Significance and Importance* (Rosthern, Sask., Canada: n.p., n.d.), p. 19. Along with "reflexive purification," Byers, in the most detailed list of the symbolisms of baptism, cites the following: (1) visible induction and seal of discipleship; (2) official ratification and witness; (3) initiation to the priesthood [of believers]; (4) token of the new dispensation of Christ; (5) prediction of our own resurrection. In *Christian Baptism* (pp. 63–74), H. M. Riggle compiled a list of baptism's significations: (1) induction into Christ; (2) spiritual rebirth; (3) quickening into life eternal; (4) death to sin; (5) Christ's death and resurrection; and (6) the believer's future resurrection.

21. Byers, ibid.

22. Byrum, *Christian Theology*, p. 576.

23. See Kenneth Renfrow's thesis for the results of his survey of Church of God ministers on their practice of baptism. Bibliographic material cited in footnote 15.

Chapter 4B

1. G. R. Beasley-Murray, "Baptism," *The New International Dictionary of New Testament Theology*, edited by Colin Brown, 4 vols. (Grand Rapids: Zondervan, 1967), 1:143–50.

Chapter 5

1. Robert Richardson, *Memoirs of Alexander Campbell* (Cincinnati: Standard, 1913), 1:236 ff.

2. Ibid., p. 63.

3. Lester G. McAllister, *Thomas Campbell: Man of the Book* (St. Louis: Bethany, 1954), p. 98.

4. Alonzo W. Fortune, *Origin and Development of the Disciples of Christ* (St. Louis: Christian Board of Publication, 1924), p. 63.

5. Alexander Campbell, *The Christian System* (Bethany, W. Va.: Alexander Campbell, 1839), p. 81.

6. McAllister, op. cit., p. 153.

7. Campbell, *The Christian System*, p. 61–62.

8. Alexander Campbell and John Walker, *Infant Sprinkling Proved to Be a Human Tradition* (Steubenville, Ohio: James Wilson, 1820), p. 138.

9. *Millennial Harbinger*, 1835, pp. 15–16.

10. *Millennial Harbinger*, 1840, pp. 544–45.

11. *Millennial Harbinger*, 1847, p. 250.

12. *Millennial Harbinger*, 1861, pp. 327–28.

13. *Protestant Unionist*, 3:35 (August 4, 1847), 138.

14. Walter Scott, *The Messiahship; or, Great Demonstrations* (1860; reprint, Kansas City: Old Paths Book Club, 1949), p. 63.

15. O. H. Donogh, *The Gospel Restored* (1836; reprint, Kansas City: Old Paths Book Club, Kansas City, 1949), pp. 474–75.

16. *The Evangelist*, 2:8, p. 169 (cited in John W. Neth, *Walter Scott Speaks: A Handbook of Doctrine* [Milligan College, Tenn.: Emmanuel School of Religion, 1967], p. 82).

17. Lester McCallister and William E. Tucker, *Journey in Faith: A History of the Christian Church (Disciples of Christ)* (St. Louis: Bethany, 1975), p. 157.

18. Ibid.

19. James DeForrest Murch, *Christians Only: A History of the Restoration Movement* (Cincinnati: Standard, 1962), p. 93.

20. Charles C. Ware, *Barton Warren Stone* (St. Louis: Bethany, 1932), p. 264 (quotes from *The Christian Messenger*, 7:3–6.

21. Ibid., p. 231.

22. Moses E. Lard, *Christian Quarterly*, 2 (April 1865), p. 262.

23. *Millennial Harbinger*, December 1861, p. 711.

24. McCallister and Tucker, *Journey in Faith*, p. 377.

25. Alfred Thomas DeGroot, *The Grounds of Divisions Among the Disciples of Christ* (Chicago: n.p., 1940), p. 189.

26. *The Christian-Evangelist*, September 7, 1922.

Chapter 6

1. Alexander Campbell, "Ancient Gospel—No. 1," *Christian Baptist*, 5 (January 7, 1828), 401.

2. Alexander Campbell, "Ancient Gospel—No. IV," *Christian Baptist*, 5 (April 7, 1828), 82.

3. Alexander Campbell, "Any Christians Among Protestant Bodies?" *Millennial Harbinger*, 2d ser., 1 (September 1837), 411–12.

4. John F. Rowe, "Re-Examination, No. II," *American Christian Review*, 12 (November 23, 1869), 373.

5. J. J. Moss, "Christians Among the Sects," *American Christian Review*, 5 (July 1, 1862), 3.

6. Alexander Campbell, "Notes on a Tour to Eastern Virginia, No. IV," *Millennial Harbinger*, 4th ser., 6 (May 1856), 287–92.

7. Alexander Campbell, *Christian Baptist*, 2 (September 1824), 92.

8. Mrs. Alexander Campbell, "Letters from Sister Alexander Campbell," *American Christian Review*, 22 (November 25, 1879), 379.

Chapter 7

1. Martin Luther, *Christian Liberty* (Philadelphia: Fortress, 1957), p. 31.

2. Maurice Creasey, *The Inward and the Outward in Early Quaker Language* (London: Friends Historical Society, 1962).

3. Robert Barclay, *An Apology for the True Christian Divinity* (London, 1678), prop. XI, sects. 9, 5, 6. Cf. George Gorman, *The Amazing Fact of Quaker Worship* (1973).

4. Thomas R. Kelley, *Testament of Devotion* (New York: Harper and Row, 1941), p. 46.

5. John Greenleaf Whittier, "The Meeting."

6. Barclay, *An Apology*, XI, 17.

7. Ibid., 18.

8. Isaac Penington, *Works* (1681) pt. 2, p. 105, quoted in Creasey, *The Inward and the Outward*, p. 9.

9. Cf. Eric Hayman, *Worship and the Common Life* (Cambridge: Cambridge University Press, 1944); Percy Bartlett, *Quakers and the Christian Church* (London: Faith and Order Commission of the Society of Friends, 1942).

10. Alan Kolp, mimeographed manuscript, pp. 14–16.

11. John Banks, *Journal*, (1712), pp. 4, 10–11.

12. Ibid.

13. Howard H. Brinton, *Friends for 300 Years* (New York: Harper and Row, 1952), p. 87.

14. Francis Howgill, *Dawnings of the Gospel Day* (1676), p. 424.

15. Ibid. and George Fox, *Gospel-Truth Demonstrated* (1706), pp. 1086.

16. Brinton, *Friends for 300 Years*, p. 20.

17. Barclay, *An Apology*, XIII:2.

Chapter 8

1. "Baptism, Eucharist, and Ministry" Faith and Order Paper No. 111 (Geneva: World Council of Churches, 1982).

2. *A Debate Between Rev. A. Campbell and Rev. N. L. Rice on the Action, Subject, Design, and Administration of Christian Baptism* . . . . (Lexington: T. Skillman, 1844).

3. Earl West, *To Be a Presbyterian* (Atlanta: John Knox Press, 1983).

4. Karl Barth, *Teaching of the Church Regarding Baptism*, trans. Ernest A. Payne (London: SCM, 1948); G. R. Beasley-Murray, *Baptism in the New Testament* (London: Macmillan, 1962).

5. Joachim Jeremias, *Infant Baptism in the First Four Centuries*, trans. David Cairns (Philadelphia: Westminster, 1960); Kurt Aland, *Did the Early Church Baptize Infants?*, trans. Beasley-Murray (Philadelphia: Westminster, 1961).

6. Oscar Cullmann, *Baptism in the New Testament*, trans. J. K. S. Reid (London: SCM, 1964), p. 73.

7. Geoffrey Wainwright, *Christian Initiation* (Atlanta: John Knox Press, 1969), pp. 12–13.

8. John Calvin, *Institutes of the Christian Religion*, John T. McNeill, ed. (Philadelphia: Westminster, 1960).

Chapter 10

1. "Towards an Ecumenical Consensus on Baptism, Eucharist, and the Ministry," *Faith and Order Paper No. 84* (Geneva: World Council of Churches, 1977), p. 23.

2. "Lausanne 77: Fifty Years of Faith and Order," *Faith and Order Paper No. 82* (Geneva: World Council of Churches, 1977), p. 39.

Chapter 12

1. James Hennesey, *American Catholics: A History of the Roman Catholic Community in the United States* (New York: Oxford University Press, 1981).

2. John Courtney Murray, *We Hold These Truths: Catholic Reflections on the American Proposition* (New York: Sheed and Ward, 1966).

3. *The Teachings of the Second Vatican Council* (Westminster, Md.: Newman, 1966), p. 366.

4. John Roach, "Are Christians Free?," *Origins*, 13:21 (November 3, 1984): 341.

5. *Code of Canon Law* (Washington, D.C.: Canon Law Society of America, 1983).

6. David O'Brien, "The Roman Catholic Experience in the United States," *Review and Expositor*, Issues in Southern Baptist—Roman Catholic Dialogue, 79:2 (Spring 1982).

7. Donald Durnbaugh, *The Believers' Church* (London: Macmillan, 1965), p. 32.

Baptism and Church:

8. Raymond E. Brown, "One Baptism for the Remission of Sins—New Testament Roots," *Lutherans and Catholics in Dialogue I—III*, Paul C. Empie and T. Austin Murphy, eds. (Minneapolis: Augsburg, 1965).

9. Donald Bloesch, *The Future of Evangelical Christianity: A Call for Unity Amid Diversity* (Garden City, N.Y.: Doubleday, 1983); see p. 56 for his discussion of baptism within the inter-evangelical ecumenical discussions.

10. *Louisville Consultation on Baptism*, Faith and Order Paper #97, (*Review and Expositor*, 77:1 [Winter 1980]).

11. *American Baptist Quarterly*, Lutheran—Baptist Dialogue 1:2 (December 1982); Richard Harmon, "A Reflection on Bilateral Statements Concerning Baptism, Initiation, and Membership" (available from Commission on Faith and Order, 475 Riverside Drive, New York, NY 10115).

12. Unpublished Third Draft: Response of the United Methodist Church to *Baptism, Eucharist, and Ministry*, p. 14.

13. John Coventry, "Baptist, Eucharist and Ministry: A Roman Catholic Response," *One In Christ*, 20:1 (1984).

14. David Paton, ed., *Breaking Barriers* Nairobi 1975 (London: SPCK; Grand Rapids: Eerdmans, 1976), p. 60; "Ecumenical Chronicle," *The Ecumenical Review* 26:2 (April 1974): 291–98; "Conciliar Fellowship," *Midstream* 21:2 (April 1982): 243–68; *In Each Place: Towards a Fellowship of Local Churches Truly United* (Geneva: World Council of Churches, 1977).

15. *Towards Visible Unity*, Faith and Order Paper No. 112, (Geneva: World Council of Churches, 1982); Hans-Georg Link, ed., *The Roots of Our Common Faith: Faith in the Scriptures and in the Early Church*, Faith and Order Paper No. 119 (Geneva: World Council of Churches, 1984); E. Glenn Hinson, "Towards a Common Confession of Apostolic Faith," *Ecumenical Trends* 12:7 (July/August 1983): 108–10. Briefly this project will consider three questions with three methodologies. It will ask (a) to what extent can the churches recognize the Nicene Creed (381) as an ecumenical symbol of the apostolic faith, (b) can Faith and Order provide a convergence document explicating the apostolic faith in a manner recognizable to the churches, and (c) can we see in the confessions of churches around the world a contemporary expression of the apostolic faith? The methodologies used will be (1) biblical, (2) contextual, and (3) historical.

The World Council is sponsoring three consultations on the elements of the Apostolic Faith (Father, Son, and Holy Spirit), organized around the three articles of the creed in three different contexts, at least two of which will be in the third world in preparation for its next meeting to take place in Stavanger, Norway, August, 1985.

The National Council Faith and Order Commission is undertaking studies on: (a) the language of the Nicene Creed; (this study, by the way, is strongly inclusive of the believers' church perspective, starting off with a Quaker paper; papers from this study should appear in the *Union Seminary Quarterly Review*); (b) confessing the apostolic faith from the Black Church perspective; (c) the socio-political context of the Nicene Creed and the fourth-century discussions as an example of inculturation and indigenization of the gospel message; (d) christological discussions with the Oriental Orthodox Churches; and (e) pneumatological discussions over the different understandings of East and West, pentecostal, and other churches.

16. *The Final Report* (London: SPCK, 1982); Joseph Burgess, *A History of the Exegesis of Matthew 16:17*–19 from 1781 to 1965 (Ann Arbor, Mi.: Edwards Brothers, 1976); Paul Empie, T. Austin Murphy, and Joseph Burgess, eds., *Teaching Authority and Infallibility in the Church*, Lutherans and Catholics in Dialogue VI (Minneapolis: Augsburg, 1978); Paul Empie and T. Austin Murphy, eds., *Papal Primacy and the Universal Church*, Lutherans and Catholics in Dialogue V (Minneapolis: Augsburg, 1974).

17. "Justification by Faith," U. S. Lutheran-Roman Catholic Dialogue, *Origins* 13:17 (October 6, 1983).

18. Richard Lovelace, "Are There Winds of Change at the World Council?" *Christianity Today* 27:13 (September 16, 1983): 30.

19. "Winds of Change in the World Council?" *Christianity Today* 28:7 (April 20, 1984): 10.

20. Ibid., p. 12.

21. Paulos Gregorios, William Lazareth, and Nikos Nissiotis, eds., *Does Chalcedon Divide or Unite?: Towards Convergence in Orthodox Christology* (Geneva: World Council of Churches, 1981); Lukas Vischer, ed., *Spirit of God, Spirit of Christ*, Faith and Order Paper No. 103, (London: SPCK and Geneva: World Council of Churches, 1981); *Towards a Confession of the Common Faith*, Faith and Order Paper No. 100, (Geneva: World Council of Churches, 1980); *Towards Visible Unity*, Faith and Order Paper No. 113, (Geneva: World Council of Churches, 1982).

LIST OF DONORS

The following individuals have contributed to the publica-
tion costs of this volume:

John and Ruth Albright
John H. Aukerman
Cheryl and Bernard Barton
J. W. and Dora Batdorf
Opal Bengtson
James W. Bradley
Don Brandon
Paris Capron
Forest F. Carlson
Paul E. and Lona A. Decker
Glenda Flaming
Lottie M. Franklin
Walter Froese
DeLoma Gadberry
Jerry C. Grubbs
Kenneth Hall
Ralph V. Hatch
Roger D. Hatch
Helen A. Holton
Don and Betty Jo Johnson
DonDeena Johnson
John and Gwen Johnson
Joyce Krepshaw
Leroy E. Lakey
Howard Lash

David Lewis
Dr. and Mrs. Marvin Lindemuth
Edith M. Lindenman
Gertrude Little
Maxine Loeber
Sarah Long
T. Franklin Miller
Gene and Agnes Newberry
Mr. & Mrs. Dalford Nisely
Faith E. Phile
Harold L. Phillips
Merrill and Doris Pyle
Mr. and Mrs. Robert E. Reitz
Hillery Rice
Kenneth F. Ritchart
Everell and Marcella Rockhill
Adam and Georgia Sanders
Robert N. Smith
Roscoe Snowden
Theodore A. Stoneberg
Merle D. Strege
Mr. and Mrs. D. R. Troutman
Dr. and Mrs. John M. Vayhinger
Joe K. Womack
Mr. & Mrs. E. C. Young